MW01165623

WINE

EVERYTHING YOU NEED TO KNOW ABOUT WINE FROM BEGINNER TO EXPERT

JAMES WALDORF

© Copyright 2015 - All rights reserved.

In no way is it legal to reproduce, duplicate, or transmit any part of this document in either electronic means or printed format. Recording of this publication is strictly prohibited and any storage of this document is not allowed unless with written permission from the publisher. All rights reserved.

The information provided herein is stated to be truthful and consistent, in that any liability, in terms of inattention or otherwise, by any usage or abuse of any policies, processes, or directions contained within is the solitary and utter responsibility of the recipient reader. Under no circumstances will any legal responsibility or blame be held against the publisher for any reparation, damages, or monetary loss due to the information herein, either directly or indirectly. Respective authors own all copyrights not held by the publisher.

Legal Notice:

This book is copyright protected. This is only for personal use. You cannot amend, distribute, sell, use, quote or paraphrase any part or the content within this book without the consent of the author or copyright owner. Legal action will be pursued if this is breached.

Disclaimer Notice:

Please note the information contained within this document is for educational and entertainment purposes only. Every attempt has been made to provide accurate and up to date information that is both reliable and complete. No warranties of any kind are expressed or implied. Readers acknowledge that the author is not engaging in the rendering of legal, financial, medical or professional advice.

By reading this document, the reader agrees that under no circumstances are we responsible for any losses, direct or indirect, which are incurred as a result of the use of the information contained within this document. This is including, but not limited to, errors, omissions, or inaccuracies.

TABLE OF CONTENTS

INTRODUCTION 7

CHAPTER ONE: A BRIEF HISTORY OF WINE 9

CHAPTER TWO: HOW TO RECOGNIZE A GOOD WINE 17

CHAPTER THREE: HEALTH BENEFITS OF WINE 23

CHAPTER FOUR: HEALTH RISKS OF DRINKING WINE 31

CHAPTER FIVE: SIGNIFICANCE OF WINE IN DIFFERENT RELIGIONS
....39

CHAPTER SIX: AGING OF WINE 43

CHAPTER SEVEN: WELL KNOWN WHITE GRAPE VARIETIES 47

CHAPTER EIGHT: WELL KNOWN RED GRAPE VARIETIES 55

CHAPTER NINE: WHAT YOU REALLY NEED TO KNOW ABOUT
APPELLATIONS...65

CHAPTER TEN: SPARKLING WINES...73

CHAPTER ELEVEN: FORTIFIED WINES 91

CHAPTER TWELVE: GUIDE TO SERVING TEMPERATURES 105

CHAPTER THIRTEEN: HOW TO BECOME A WINE CONNOISSEUR?
....113

CHAPTER FOURTEEN: THE RIGHT GLASS FOR THE RIGHT WINE
....121

CHAPTER FIFTEEN: LEARN HOW TO TASTE WINE LIKE AN
EXPERT 131

CHAPTER SIXTEEN: GUIDELINES ON PAIRING THE RIGHT FOOD WITH THE RIGHT WINE.. 143

CHAPTER SEVENTEEN: FIVE BASIC WINE CHARACTERISTICS .. 163

CHAPTER EIGHTEEN: HOW TO UNDERSTAND VINTAGE 169

CHAPTER NINETEEN: TOP FACTS ABOUT WINE 173

CHAPTER TWENTY: FINE AND RARE WINES 183

CHAPTER TWENTY ONE: FINE WINE VINEYARDS 197

CONCLUSION 205

BONUS! 207

INTRODUCTION

Wine has been around for a lot longer than you may imagine. Many people attribute the spread of wine across the world to the Romans. However, the oldest winery in the world was found in a cave in Armenia in 4100 BC, and remnants of fermented fruit and rice were found in China 3,000 years before that, in 7000 BC.

However, the Romans certainly did more than any other civilization to ensure that as many people as possible across the world became familiar with the pleasures of fermented grape juice. Today, there are so many wines you would never manage to taste them all, even if you lived to be 100 years old. Therefore, it can be quite bewildering when you're presented with rows of different wines in the supermarket, liquor store, or bodega.

So, how can you ensure that the wine you take home for dinner will slide down smoothly rather than taking a layer of enamel off your teeth? By learning about the characteristics of the various grapes and their growing conditions, that's how. This book aims to teach you all you need to know about wine and how to master the art of selection so that each bottle you open is a pleasure on the palate.

We're not going to get bogged down with rules for pairing wine with different foods and stuff like that because the only rule there should be that you enjoy every bottle you open. If you prefer red wine with fish or white wine with beef, then go for it. If you'd rather have a sweet wine than a dry wine, it doesn't mean you have an uneducated palate – it just means that you know what you like. So junk the wine snobbery and prepare to learn and enjoy as we take a fascinating journey through the wines of the world.

CHAPTER ONE

A BRIEF HISTORY OF WINE

Wine has been around since at least 7000 BC as shown by residues of fermented fruit, rice, and honey that were discovered in China. Fast forward 3,000 years, to what is believed to be the world's oldest winery, found in a cave in Armenia. There is also evidence that grapes were being cultivated in Mesopotamia from around 6000 BC, but the first real evidence of wine production on a commercial scale comes from the Phoenicians in around 3000 BC. In fact, the Phoenician word for wine, *cherem*, refers specifically to a drink produced from grapes.

Biblical references to wine abound, and some experts believe that Cana, where Jesus turned water into wine at a wedding, is located near Tyre in Phoenicia. The Canaanites were also avid wine drinkers, and there are records of people dying from drinking too much strong wine. Obviously nothing is new!

Interestingly, most wine was drunk at the table and was diluted with water. It was only at religious rites that pure, unadulterated wine was consumed. This led to a state of inebriation that was thought of by some as a spiritual state, since it coincided with rituals. Drunks were thought to be able to communicate with deities, and act as earthly channels for them. During these early years, it wasn't considered a disgrace to be drunk.

The Phoenicians exported wine all across the Mediterranean region, particularly to Egypt, where conditions did not favor viticulture. This meant that all the wine drunk in Egypt was imported from the Phoenicians, although Greece and other countries in Europe got into viticulture over the next two or three thousand years. The Romans even managed to take vines to Britain, leading to the point in time that wine production and consumption really began to spread.

Wine was the main export of the Phoenicians, and it was carried in jars called amphorae. At first, these didn't have any form of sealant, and flies and oxygen got into the wine, so they came up with the idea of floating a layer of olive oil on top. This kept the insects and oxygen out, but it was no protection in rough seas, and lots of wine ended up seasoning the ship's timbers rather than gracing the dining tables in the Mediterranean region.

Clearly, the wine had to be properly sealed, and at first discs of wood were inserted into the necks of the jars, using a resin compound to seal them in place. Soon after, the discs became cork, still using the resin, which flavored the wine, and was also thought to act as a preservative. To this day, Greek Retsina wine is still stored in barrels with resin plugs.

The earliest evidence of winemaking in Greece dates from around 1600 BC on Crete, and it seems clear that this stemmed from the Phoenicians too.

If you think drinking games are a modern thing, think again. The Greeks had a game where they used to throw the remnants of a cup of wine in the air and try to catch it on a dish balanced on a pole. Just like people today coach each other on the best way to clear levels in video games, the Greeks used to train each other to catch the tossed wine.

Wines were also produced on Cyprus, which was a Phoenician colony, from around 3000 BC. Again, there are Biblical references in the Song of Solomon. Cypriot wines were a major source of income for the island, through its export to Greece, Rome, and Egypt. Even Homer spoke of the quality of Cypriot wines.

Italy may currently be the largest wine producer in the world, but it was not always so. Like many other Mediterranean countries, the Romans developed their love of wine from the Phoenicians. The Romans were pragmatists above all else, and when they latched on to a good idea, they developed it to suit their own tastes and ideals. Once they had perfected the art of viticulture and wine production from the Phoenicians, they spread the love to France, Spain, the rest of Italy, and other parts of Europe, including Great Britain.

It was the Romans who turned wine from something to be enjoyed only by the rich and privileged to a source of pleasure for the masses. There were bars to serve all classes, and even slaves could enjoy what would today be classed as wine vinegar, diluted with water. The Romans had a sweet palate and flavored their wines with honey, flowers, and herbs and spices; they particularly favored mint. Bizarrely, they were also known to flavor wines with garlic, onions, and even fermented fish sauce.

Spain is also well known for its wine production today, and recent archaeological discoveries in the region of Valdepeñas indicate that wine was being produced there from at least 700 BC. It seems likely that the grapes used were Tempranillo, Pinot Noir, and Cabernet Sauvignon. Analysis of the finds is still going on, but it seems obvious that Spain was involved in viticulture from a much earlier date than was first suspected. There is even evidence that Mallorca was producing wine even before that, during the time when the Phoenicians were spreading viticulture around the Mediterranean region.

So, wine production in Europe was well established from the earliest times, but what about the New World wines that are so well regarded today? Simply put, New World wines are any wines that are produced outside of Europe and the Mediterranean region. So America, South America, Australia, New Zealand, and South Africa count as New World wines.

These New World wines are making a dramatic impact on the wine industry today. Australia has been producing wine for around 175 years, but it's only in the last 20 years or so that it has been recognized for the quality of its wines. These days, South Australia's Penfold Grange wine, produced from Shiraz grapes, is one of the most expensive and sought-after reds in the world.

New Zealand has been producing wines for around 200 years, but, like Australia, it took a while to find its niche. Today, Hawkes Bay Chardonnay and Marlborough Sauvignon Blanc are very much sought after, although New Zealand is a relatively small producer by world standards. New Zealand wines tend to be strongly flavored, with herbaceous notes, and are often heavily oaked.

South Africa has been producing wine for around 350 years, and it now ranks eighth in the league of world wine producers. South African wines tend to share similarities with European wines, as many of the growers studied viticulture in France. Stellenbosch, near Cape Town, is considered to be the finest producer of South African wines.

Wine came to Chile and other parts of South America in the 1500s, when Spanish and Portuguese missionaries planted vines to produce wines for the sacrament. After Spanish rule came to an end in 1810, the Chileans imported vines from Bordeaux and other famous wine regions. Ironically, following the phylloxera outbreak of 1870 which destroyed 75% of France's vineyards, Europe looked to Chile, which had escaped the outbreak, for new young plants to graft onto their phylloxera-resistant rootstocks. Almost 150 years on, Chile is one of the few countries that still have flourishing ungrafted European vines.

California's first commercial winery – Buena Vista – opened in 1870, although it would be 1976 before Californian wines found a place on the world stage. This was due to the so-called 'Judgment of Paris,' when British wine merchant Steven Spurrier organized a blind tasting in which Californian wines won in each category against French wines. As was the case in Chile, wine came to North America with Spanish missionaries. By 1890,

Zinfandel was the most popular grape in America, and today California is still best known for its wines from Zinfandel grapes.

Other important milestones in the history of wine are 1830 when the modern wine bottle shape that is now so familiar was first introduced, and 1964, when wine boxes first made an appearance. The world of wine has certainly undergone some changes since 4100 BC, the date that the first winery found in an Armenian cave was dated to. One can't help but wonder what the future holds for the world's oldest alcoholic beverage.

CHAPTER TWO

HOW TO RECOGNIZE A GOOD WINE

There are so many different wines available: reds, whites, roses, sparkling wines, fortified wines, dessert wines, etc. It can be a real headache trying to settle on something that suits both your palate and your budget. Unfortunately, there is no rule that says that the cheaper wines are rubbish, or that the most expensive ones are the best. And contrary to popular belief, age isn't always the best indicator, because not all wines improve with age. Then there's the thorny question of vintages, and which years are better than others and why. It's enough to drive you to drink, isn't it?

At one time, if a wine bottle had a screw top, it was a wine to avoid, but these days, it isn't necessarily so. Wines that are intended to be drunk while still young often have a screw top, and corks are not always made out of cork these days. So, how can you tell whether a certain wine is a good buy or not even fit for cooking with? Here are a few pointers to help you make the right choices when it comes to wine – whatever the color or variety.

READ THE FLIP SIDE

That fancy label on the front of the bottle isn't any indication of the quality of the contents, although it will tell you the grape variety and the year of bottling. Turn the bottle around, and read the information on the flip side. That's where you'll find tasting notes, and the region the grapes are grown in, as well as how long the wine has been aged, and how. If you're not a fan of heavily oaked wines, steer clear of Californian wines and some Chardonnays. Pinot Noir is often oak-aged too. Oaked wines don't tend to have the fruity, fresh taste of the grape, although they will taste full and rounded in the mouth. You should be able to find this out from the back label.

The alcohol content is also a good indication of how the wine is likely to sit on the palate. Look for an alcohol content of 12% alcohol by volume (ABV) or less for a more balanced flavor. If you're looking for a light, fruity taste, go for wine that's less than two years old.

If the wine is estate bottled, it will say so on the label, and that's another good pointer. It means the people who made the wine also grew the grapes, so they have a lot invested in their product and are more likely to produce wines of consistent quality.

The back label will also tell you about any awards the wine has won, as well as highlighting good reviews. If it's an award winner, or it has five-star reviews, it's going to be something pretty special. That's not to say that wines that haven't won awards aren't good, just that an award is an extra clue to excellence.

BRUSH UP ON YOUR GEOGRAPHY

Some wine regions produce better wines than others, due to soil properties, temperature, sunshine hours, grape varieties, and all sorts of other factors. Even in well-known wine producing regions, some areas will consistently deliver a better product than others. If you want a good Spanish red, you can't do much better than a wine produced in the Rioja province in Northern Spain. Just like if you like Californian wines, you'll love wines from the Napa Valley.

If you were after a slightly sweeter, fruity white wine, you'd go for a Moscato (or Muscat) from the Rhone Valley in France or

Italy. It's worth doing a little research to find out which areas produce the style of wine you prefer.

PRICE

As has already been noted, the price isn't necessarily a guideline for quality. However, say there are two Merlots, and one is priced at $5, and the other is $10. It's a pretty good bet that the cheaper Merlot is likely to be a little heavy on the tannin while the more expensive one should be softer on the palate.

Don't go for the cheapest, but it's not necessary to go for the most expensive either. A great way to find a good wine is to check out the sale offers on the grape varieties you enjoy. Often, more expensive wines are discounted by as much as 50%, so keep an eye on the shelf stickers, and get yourself a bargain. Check out the label too though, to make sure you're buying what you want to drink. Never let price be your main influence, whether high or low end, because you're almost certain to be disappointed if you do.

GRAPE VARIETY

Even if you're not too well versed in grape varieties, if you read up a little on the taste characteristics, you'll get to recognize the flavors and aromas you like, and that should help you make your choices. You'll always get the best match to your preferences if you choose a single grape variety wine, but that may not always be possible, and you may have to settle for a blend.

The problem with blends is you can't be sure of the ratio, and how it will affect the end product. What may suit the wine maker may not suit your palate, so it pays to make a note of the blends you may or may not find acceptable. If you're not a fan of **dry white wines**, you may want to avoid blends containing Sauvignon Blanc, Pinot Grigio, and Reisling. It's worth putting the time into research to determine which of the various grape varieties suits your taste.

The tips above should ensure that you don't return from the supermarket or liquor store with a bottle of paint thinner or worse, but what happens when you open the bottle? How can you tell whether you have a good bottle of wine or just a flop?

AROMA

A wine should smell pleasant, even if it doesn't smell like they say it should on the label. Everyone's nose is different, and different people pick up different aromas. However, if something doesn't smell right, it's likely that the wine won't taste right to you, because somewhere, the balance will be wrong. It's difficult to be more specific on this, but after you've smelled a few different bottles of wine, you'll get the picture, and learn to distinguish between a decent bottle of wine and something you don't want to proceed any further with, even before you taste it.

BALANCE

Balance has been mentioned a couple of times, in terms of alcohol content and aroma. Basically, if when you taste the wine, something stands out as not quite right, then the balance is wrong. The majority of wines will have a good balance for most people. If the sweetness, acidity, alcohol, and tannin levels are in harmony, you've got yourself a nicely balanced wine and all is right with the world. However, if there is too much or too little sweetness, or if the wine tastes acidic or flat, or a bit heavy due to tannin overload, maybe it's not the right wine for you.

How do you know if there's too much tannin or alcohol? Well, first, you'll get a quick hit on the tongue, and then the taste will fade very quickly. If it lingers, and you can taste it all around your mouth, your wine is nicely balanced.

Clearly, any discussion about good wines will be subjective, once you get past the label and the facts since everyone's tastes are different. However, these guidelines should help you to choose a wine you enjoy – and any wine you enjoy is a good wine, regardless of its provenance or price.

CHAPTER THREE

HEALTH BENEFITS OF WINE

A HEALTHIER HEART

Drinking a moderate amount of wine is shown to be quite beneficial to the heart. It reduces the risk of cardiovascular diseases and the occurrence of heart attacks. Studies have shown that wine drinkers have a lower death rate caused by heart related problems as compared to those who do not drink wine. Drinking wine in moderation seems to reduce the risk of a heart-related untimely death by almost one-third in comparison to those who abstain from wine. Due to this, there are increasing numbers of studies and research being conducted to understand exactly how wine benefits the heart.

For instance, it is seen that the risk of blood clots decreases because wine helps to dilate the arteries and thus increase the flow of blood. This helps in preventing damage to heart muscles and avoiding blood supply problems. The levels of "good" cholesterol or HDL are also increased by wine consumption and this prevents damage to the arteries that are usually caused by bad cholesterol, or LDL. Wine in the system helps to prevent the clogging of arteries due to excessive bad cholesterol. The phenols in wine also help in this particular function of working against damage due to LDL's.

AGAINST CANCER

Cancer is yet another evil against which wine seems to work. Several properties in wine allow it to work on the body in a way that helps to protect against some forms of cancer.

For instance, the phenols in red wine are said to slow down the growth of cancerous cells in breast cancer. While most forms of alcohol actually increase the risk of this type of cancer, red wine works in the opposite manner. Certain compounds in wine increase the levels of testosterone in women thus lowering their risk of developing breast cancer. Other types of alcohol increase the estrogen levels instead and thus increase the risk of breast cancer. The main compounds that actually benefit this purpose are present in the red grapes used for making this alcoholic beverage.

The risk of colon cancer or bowel tumors is also reduced significantly in those who drink red wine in moderation. When studies were conducted to check the occurrence of prostate cancer, however, it was seen to occur as frequently in wine drinkers as non-wine drinkers.

The risk of lung cancer is also less in those who drink red wine as compared to those who don't. The antioxidant properties of red wine work to protect against lung cancer and is especially helpful for smokers who have higher risks of developing this disease.

Red wine has also shown to be protective against oral cancer, as demonstrated by some studies. The antioxidant quercetin and the resveratrol in wine inhibit the growth of cancer cells. Many such properties of red wine work in boosting the body's immunity helping it to resist cancer.

AGAINST DEPRESSION

While drinking in excess can lead to depression, it is observed that drinking wine in moderation can help in reducing the risk of depression. This was seen based on a study that observed how much wine men and women drink on a weekly basis. Those who consumed a glass of wine a day had a lower frequency of being diagnosed with depression.

ANTI-AGING EFFECT

Red wine is also said to have anti-aging effects. This has been talked about since ancient times and has been recorded throughout history in several communities. Many attribute the long lifespan of monks in comparison to the common folk of Europe to the fact that they drank more wine. The compound in wine, which is said to have this anti-aging effect, is known as resveratrol. Another factor is the procyanidins, which benefit blood vessels. Due to such properties, the wine drinking habit is said to increase the life span of people compared to those who do not consume any.

AGAINST DEMENTIA

Some researchers have found that drinking certain amounts of wine helps in reducing the risk of dementia in people. Compared to those who drink wine, non-drinkers have shown a higher risk of developing dementia. The compound resveratrol, which is obtained from the skin of grapes, is what helps the blood vessels stay flexible and provide adequate blood to the brain.

AGAINST BLINDNESS

Drinking red wine is also beneficial in working against blindness. When the growth of blood vessels gets out of control it leads to blindness in the person. This overgrowth gives rise to conditions like diabetic retinopathy, which causes age related blindness. The resveratrol in wine helps in protecting vision.

PROTECTS BRAIN

The brain is very susceptible to damage after a stroke. Red wine has even been said to protect the brain against this damage. Resveratrol from the wine helps to increase the levels of the enzyme heme oxygenase. This enzyme is what protects the nerve cells after the person suffers a stroke. This enzyme must already be present in an elevated level prior to the stroke, or it will have no effect. Doctors strongly caution that those who are at an elevated risk of stroke should carefully weigh the risks of consuming alcohol with the potential benefits.

BENEFITS LUNGS

White wine is observed to have a higher rate of positive effects on lung function in comparison to those drinking red wine. While red wine itself does not seem to show any obvious effect, the compound resveratrol is beneficial in its pure form. A study showed that moderate wine drinkers usually have better lung function than others. However, when it comes to the risk of lung cancer, an antioxidant in red wine works protectively.

AGAINST LIVER DISEASE

The risk of getting fatty liver disease is reduced by half in those who drink moderate amounts of wine as compared to those who don't. This sounds a little against the grain when you consider the effect alcohol usually has on the liver. However, those who drink other types of alcoholic drinks such as whiskey were found to be more at risk for fatty liver disease.

AGAINST DIABETES

Resveratrol from wine has shown to improve the insulin sensitivity in the body. Type 2 diabetes is greatly due to insulin resistance. Hence, drinking red wine goes quite a long way in preventing the occurrence of this disease. Although many studies are still being conducted with research to prove the actual validity of these observations, red wine has still shown promising effects with relation to type 2 diabetes prevention.

STRONGER BONES

Recent research has shown that people who consume red wine in moderate amounts also cut down the risk of developing osteoporosis. This disease occurs over time due to loss of calcium in bone. However, wine-drinking women demonstrated higher density of bone minerals than those who do did not consume wine or drank too much. The bone strength in these moderate wine-drinking people was determined to be higher than those who did not drink or drank too much.

RESVERATROL

Since you have seen how frequently this particular term was associated with the beneficial effects of wine, take a deeper look into it.

Resveratrol is part of the polyphenol plant compounds group. It has antioxidant properties that help to protect the body from risks of diseases like cancer or heart conditions. The anti-aging properties of this are also quite significant.

It helps in the following ways:

- Prevents clots from forming due to LDL oxidation. This helps in protecting against heart diseases.
- Protects nerve cells from suffering damage and leading up to other diseases.
- Increases insulin sensitivity and decreases insulin resistance. This helps to act against the occurrence of diabetes.
- Good sources of resveratrol are:
- Blueberries
- Dark chocolate
- Raspberries

- Peanuts
- Red wine

  •Red Grapes

CHAPTER FOUR

HEALTH RISKS OF DRINKING WINE

When looking at the positives, you have to remember that there are also negatives that need to be considered. This is especially true when it comes to the consumption of alcohol. Alcohol consumption is often discouraged due to the fact that more often than not, it is abused. However, there are positive aspects or benefits that can be reaped if it is consumed in moderate amounts. As you have read above, wine can have quite a few beneficial effects on the body if it is taken in moderate amounts while following a healthy lifestyle. Keeping those health benefits in mind, take a look at the hazards of wine consumption as well.

ALCOHOL ABUSE

One of the most negative side effects of consuming alcohol is that it is abused too frequently. For most people, consuming wine in moderate amounts will not harm the body and can offer health benefits. Like any form of alcohol, consuming wine in large quantities and too frequently will lead to addiction. Like all addictions, these tendencies will lead up to the destruction of mental, financial, and physical health. The ramifications of wine addiction can cause too many negative changes in your body. The worst part is that this kind of addiction affects not only you but those near you as well.

SLEEP

Consuming too much wine can make you feel quite drowsy or sleepy. This is because the alcohol moves through the body directly into the bloodstream and thus reduces cellular activity. Having just a little wine can be okay but too much will prevent restful sleep.

HEART PROBLEMS

Moderation is the key word if you want to reap the beneficial effects of drinking red wine. If you go beyond that moderate amount of consumption that is recommended, it becomes detrimental. Too much wine will increase the heart rate and amount of blood that is pumped out. It puts excessive stress on the circulatory system and also affects nerve activity. While a little wine is good for the heart, too much can increase the risk of heart attacks and increased blood pressure. Drinking too much red wine in a day can lead up to hypertension, strokes, cardiomyopathy, etc.

DENTAL ISSUES

Sensitive teeth can be affected quite negatively by wine. Wine contains acid that will cause the enamel to wear away over time. With the loss of enamel, wine also makes the teeth more prone to decay. Do not brush your teeth right after drinking wine, however, as it is even more aggravating on the teeth.

ALLERGIES

People with allergies need to be careful of what they consume. There are different components in wine that can cause an allergic reaction in your body if you are susceptible to them. For instance, those who suffer from asthma should be more wary since the sulfite content in wine is quite high. Allergic reactions can cause nausea and hives in such people and death via anaphylactic shock.

WEIGHT ISSUES

People who are obese or have any excessive weight should also be cautious of drinking alcohol. In such cases drinking wine can actually add to unwanted body weight due to the triglycerides and empty calories. Drinking too much wine is also linked to increased eating and decreased physical activity. This inadvertently leads to more weight gain. A couple of glasses of wine can add up to a few hundred calories quickly which is a significant portion of your recommended daily intake.

MIGRAINES

Wine also seems to work as a migraine trigger, therefore, people prone to migraines should be cautious.

PANCREATITIS

Acute pancreatitis can occur if the intake of alcohol is excessive. Although it is not guaranteed that every person will develop such issues, the majority have shown a tendency towards it. Too much wine or any alcohol can also aggravate chronic pancreatitis.

PREGNANCY

Pregnant women always need to be much more cautious about their health than others. They need to remember that anything they do will also affect the child they carry. Alcohol in any form should be avoided during pregnancy as it can cause problems in the development of the child or even be fatal. The effects of alcohol on unborn children can affect them both physically as well as mentally and thus lead to many issues after birth. Drinking alcohol is also to be avoided when a woman is breastfeeding. This is because the alcohol content could pass into the breast milk and this will harm the child. The production of milk in the woman is also reduced if too much wine is consumed.

LIVER PROBLEMS

Abusing alcohol more often than not leads to problems in the liver. The liver needs to work overtime to compensate for the excessive amounts of alcohol being consumed. With the liver focusing on filtering out the alcohol, it can make the body more susceptible to diseases, infections, cirrhosis, and complete dysfunction as well. This is why large quantities of alcohol can very quickly show detrimental effects on the liver.

REACTIONS WITH OTHER DRUGS

If you are on other prescription drugs, make sure to check if it is okay to be consuming alcohol. Even the wine that you drink moderately may react negatively with the medications that you are taking. It could also work against the purpose of the drugs that have been prescribed and thus negate any benefits from the medication altogether.

GERD

Gastroesophageal reflux disease or stomach ulcers are worsened by consumption of alcohol regardless of how much is consumed.

FERTILITY

Increased intake of alcohol decreases the testosterone levels in males. It also causes erectile dysfunction and reduces motility of the sperms. This is why abstaining from alcohol can be beneficial when a couple is trying to conceive. Excessive alcohol in the body can also cause fertility issues in women including a higher risk of miscarriages.

As you can see, there are a huge number of problems that are associated with drinking wine or any other alcohol. A certain amount can be potentially beneficial; however, more often than not excessive consumption of alcohol causes various health issues over time. These illnesses could be physiological in nature such as cancers or organ diseases. They could also be psychological in nature such as depression, Alzheimer's, and other such problems. The negative effects can quickly outweigh the positive effects when it comes to wine consumption. Therefore, it is important to weigh these risks and know when and how much alcohol consumption is feasible for your body.

CHAPTER FIVE

SIGNIFICANCE OF WINE IN DIFFERENT RELIGIONS

Wine and religion have a long-standing association that has been indicated over time. The role of wine has been found to be very significant in various religions all over the world.

CHRISTIANITY

Amongst all the religions, wine probably has the most prominent place in Christianity. It is a very important symbol in the church, and there are references to wine in most Biblical stories. One of the most famous stories is that of Jesus Christ turning water into wine as depicted in the New Testament. The significance of wine is emphasized even more as Jesus Christ is said to have shared wine and bread with his disciples in the Last Supper. Due to such events and stories, wine as well as bread are used as symbols to represent the blood and the body of Christ, the Son of God. The Holy Communion ceremony is conducted using sacramental wine. However, some denominations allow the consumption of wine while others oppose it.

JUDAISM

Wine is also considered significant in Judaism. It is associated to divinity and is part of several of their rituals. In fact, the Hebrew Bible has passages that emphasize the importance of wine where they threaten barren fruit if their followers sin. Jewish holidays are sanctified with the wine being blessed. There are certain ceremonies like the Passover where the followers are obligated to drink a few glasses of wine. At times, wine is also part of sacrificial services. Some laws of Judaism also dictate how the wine should be produced, this type of wine referred to as kosher wine.

ISLAM

Although Islam is quite similar to Christianity and Judaism, it differs in its opinion of alcohol. The consumption of any form of alcohol, including wine, is forbidden under Islamic laws. Before the Islamic revolution or the birth of Muhammad, wine was quite popular in the Middle East. The Qur'an had quite a few teachings when it came to alcohol. While wine was considered a gift from God, the consumption was later forbidden because of how people abused it and behaved irreligiously after that. However, not all Muslims obey this prohibition. However, in the Middle Eastern countries which follow Islam, there have often been laws passed in order to make this prohibition more effective.

HINDUISM

In Hinduism, consumption of wine is considered a sin. However, over time, this restriction was placed only on the highest caste or division known as the Brahmins. The people from lower castes were given more leniencies in consuming such drinks.

BUDDHISM

Another widely practiced religion, Buddhism prohibits the consumption of wine or any alcohol. The teaching of Lord Buddha is aimed towards attaining enlightenment, and this is hindered with alcohol consumption. However, some sects allow wine consumption, as they believe it assists in achieving an enlightened state. Similarly, the rules on alcohol consumption have varied amongst Buddhists in different places.

CHAPTER SIX

AGING OF WINE

The basic idea here is to store some wine over a period of time in a controlled environment and allow it to age. While most of the things we consume spoil over time and certain wines do the same, high-quality wines get better with age. The wine is kept in a dark and cool place for years to improve the taste. The allure of drinking aged wine is even greater for a true lover of wine or wine connoisseur. The texture and flavor of the wine undergoes a drastic change when it is allowed to age.

The "cellaring" of wine has been practiced since ancient times and is an art in and of itself. In the past, wine was stored in earthenware, catacombs, etc. However, over time, different methods of storing wine to prevent it from perishing were developed. The discovery of the cork and bottle were very significant in improving the wine industry.

However, you need to keep in mind that not all wine can be aged in order to improve it. Most of the wine we buy is actually meant for immediate consumption and will quickly spoil if left too long. Only a small percentage of the wine produced around the world can be stored and kept for aging. This does not mean that new and cheap wine tastes bad while old wine is the only good option. They are just different. Keeping a new bottle of wine in storage for the next ten years is more likely to spoil it than to improve its taste.

The wine's ability to age will depend on a number of factors starting from the variety of grapes and the region where it was grown to the process of making the wine. The suitability of creating a wine to age is more in favor of those that have a lower pH and higher phenol level. Some such wines are the Pinot Noir and Cabernet Sauvignon. The most important factors in cellaring wine is controlling the temperature, light, humidity, etc. of the place it is stored. If you can control these and have the right kind of wine, they will definitely age well. However, finding a bottle of wine with good aging potential is rarer than you would expect.

WINES WITH GOOD AGING POTENTIAL ARE:

- Chardonnay
- Riesling

- Syrah
- Merlot
- Cabernet sauvignon
- Zinfandel
- Nebbiolo, etc.

WINES WITH BAD AGING POTENTIAL ARE:
- Sherry
- Tawny port
- Box wine
- Nouveau wine
- Asti
- Rose wine, etc.

CHAPTER SEVEN

WELL KNOWN WHITE GRAPE VARIETIES

There are three main types of wine: red, white, and rose. And there are two types of grape: those with white (or green) skins and those with black (or red) skins. For the purposes of clarity, we'll just refer to them as red and white grapes. Rose wines are produced from red grapes, and the color is determined by the length of time the skins remain in the must.

There are around 10,000 varieties of grapes used in winemaking, although a number of these are clones of other grapes, and may be called by different names in different countries. Some experts put the number of grape varieties that are used in commercial wine production at around 1,300, but you'll be relieved to know that we don't intend to produce an exhaustive list here. However, the aim of this book is to educate and inform, so we'll take a close look at the more well known varieties of grapes, where they're likely to be grown, and what sort of wine you can expect to enjoy from them.

CHARDONNAY

In recent years, it's become popular as a girl's name, and Chardonnay is possibly the most well know white grape variety there is. Even people who know nothing about wine are familiar with the term Chardonnay. This is why when people are taking a bottle of wine to a dinner party or for a gift, they'll often settle on Chardonnay.

Chardonnay is the grape used in white Burgundies, which are arguably the best white wines in the world. It's also used in many types of champagne, and is grown all over the world since it can successfully adapt to most climates. Growers like to grow Chardonnay grapes because they know they will thrive almost anywhere, and they know their wines will sell if it says Chardonnay on the label.

Flavor wise, Chardonnay is rather full-bodied, with fruity overtones that depend on the climate the grape is grown in. In cooler countries, you may notice the taste and flavor of apple whereas grapes grown in warmer climates tend to produce tropical fruit flavors such as pineapple in the finished wine.

Chardonnay is often oaked to a greater or lesser degree. This can happen during or after fermentation. Depending on the quality of the wine, Chardonnay can be aged in oak barrels, or oak chips or oak essence may be added to the wine. If you're not a fan of oaked wines, steer clear of Chardonnay. It's also a dry wine, although cheaper Chardonnays tend to be a little sweeter.

Most Chardonnays are at their best when drunk within five years of bottling. However, the best white Burgundies are still good to go after 10 years or more. It's down to personal preference really. The younger the wine, the fruitier the flavor.

RIESLING

Riesling is another grape that generally produces a dry white wine, although there are sweeter varieties emerging on an increasing scale. Unlike Chardonnay, the Riesling grape does not travel well. The best wines from Riesling are likely to come from Germany, with the Alsace region in France, Austria, and the Clare Valley in Australia also producing good quality wines. Look out for Rieslings from Mosel-Saar-Ruwer, Rheinhessen, and Rheingau in Germany. Some American Rieslings are also worth trying.

If you're looking for a light, fruity, or flowery tasting wine that's low on alcohol content but fairly high in acidity, maybe a

Riesling is for you. German Rieslings tend to be dry, and will say *trocken* on the label. *Halbtrocken*, literally 'half dry,' means the wine is medium dry. If you're not used to Rieslings or very dry white wines, it may be better to start with a halbtrocken. Sylvaner grapes produce similar wines to Rieslings.

SAUVIGNON BLANC

As the name may suggest, Sauvignon Blanc is a classic French grape. It produces a dry wine, and if you don't like your wines oaked, you might find this more to your taste, since usually it's left unoaked. The wines produced from Sauvignon Blanc grapes tend to have fruity or herbaceous flavors, depending on the region they are grown in. They tend to be high in acidity, with distinctive flavors. In blind tastings, Sauvignon Blancs are usually easier to single out than other varieties.

In France, the main regions for growing Sauvignon Blanc grapes are the Loire Valley and Bordeaux. If you buy a Sancerre or Pouille-Fume, it will have come from one of these classic wine-producing regions. Some producers in Bordeaux blend Sauvignon Blanc with Semillon grapes.

Sauvignon Blanc grapes are also grown in Italy, South Africa, and areas of California. The wines from these regions may be labeled as Fume Blanc. New Zealand also produces some good Sauvignon Blanc wines.

PINOT GRIS/ PINOT GRIGIO

There are several Pinot varieties of grape, of which Pinot Gris, or Pinot Grigio as it's known in Italy, is probably the best known. The others are Pinot Blanc, Pinot Noir, and Pinot Meunier. Pinot Gris is believed to be a mutation of Pinot Noir, and its skin is certainly rather dark for a white wine producing grape. This often produces a deeper colored wine, although Italian Pinot Grigios are typically pale. These wines are medium bodied and low in acidity, with no overpowering flavors or aromas. They are also unoaked and relatively inexpensive. Sometimes there is a hint of fruit skins in the bouquet and the flavor.

Pinot Gris grapes are grown in the Alsace region of France, California, Germany and Oregon. North Eastern Italy is a major producer of Pinot Grigio. Pinot Blanc and Chenin Blanc wines are often similar in style to those made from Pinot Grigio.

GEWURZTRAMINER

Okay, this German grape is a bit of a mouthful, but it produces an excellent wine that pairs really well with Asian and spicy foods such as curries. If you've often fancied a wine to go with a curry, but thought the spices in the food would overpower it, you should try a Gewurztraminer. The prefix 'gewurz' actually means spicy in German, so that's a good indication of what you can pair it with. It also goes well with smoked cheeses.

Wines produced from these grapes range from slightly dry to sweet, with unusual aromas and flavors. You'll notice touches of ginger, maybe even lychees and rosewater. The best Gewurztraminers come from Germany and Alsace, although Spain is beginning to produce some excellent options.

MUSCAT/MOSCATO/MUSCATEL

If you prefer a sweeter white wine, look for one made from the Muscat grape, also called Moscato in Italy and Muscatel in Spain. It's a really old grape variety, having been around since classical times. In fact, this grape variety has almost been around as long as wine itself. There are around 200 types of Muscat, and the best ones are small with yellow skins, although the colors can vary significantly. An Australian variety called Brown Muscat makes an excellent wine. That's most likely the grape the Romans imported into their colonies, and it makes a sweet, dark wine that is very much still enjoyed in many places, particularly Greece.

In fact, all Muscats make wines that taste and smell mainly of grapes. In Italy, they're used to make slightly sparkling Moscato d'Asti, which tends to be low in alcohol content at around 5% ABV. Muscats tend to be used for sweeter wines and dessert wines. Some Muscats, particularly those from Spain, can be rather sickly sweet. It's certainly a wine where it doesn't pay to go for the cheapest.

VERDEJO

Verdejo is mainly used in white wines from Rueda, in Spain. The grape is thought to have originated in North Africa, coming into the Castille y Leon region of Spain back in the 11th century. It went out of favor for several hundred years, but was revived in the 1980s, and is considered by some experts to be Spain's best white grape. It's grown mainly in Rueda, although it is also seen in Australia and California.

Verdejo is a grape that produces crisp, dry white wines with a nutty flavor, even from poor quality soils and a very dry climate. It's often blended with Sauvignon Blanc. Look out for Rueda Superior, an excellent white wine made with 85% Verdejo grapes.

SEMILLON

Semillon grapes are grown in the Bordeaux area of France, and also in New World countries such as Chile, Argentina, Australia, and California. Semillon is the third grape in terms of importance in France, after Sauvignon Blanc and Chardonnay. It has a rather unusual flavor, reminiscent of figs and grass, and is rarely used alone. It's often harvested while unripe and blended with Sauvignon Blanc. A specialty of the Bordeaux region is ripe Semillon grapes blended with Sauvignon Blanc to produce a high quality, full-bodied sweet Sauternes. Semillon also features in white Bordeaux wines.

As far as flavor goes, Semillon wines have notes of citrus, especially when under-ripe, when they also have more acidity. Typical of this is Hunter Valley Semillon from Australia.

Here, we have merely touched on some of the more popular and common white grapes used in the world's favorite wines. It's really no good trying to take too much information on board, as it will just confuse you. And if you're familiar with the main white grape varieties, you can also acquaint yourself with other, similar varieties. Now let's take a look at some of the most famous and popular red grape varieties.

CHAPTER EIGHT

WELL KNOWN RED GRAPE VARIETIES

The main difference between red grapes and white grapes, apart from the obvious color thing, is the variety of taste experiences in the wines produced from them. There seem to be much more dramatic differences in the flavors of red wines than whites. In fact, if you're new to wine tasting, you may have to try a number of different reds before you find something you really like.

The tannin content of red wine is largely responsible for these variations. Put simply, tannins are found in the stems, seeds, and skins of grapes, and although there are tannins in white grapes, there are a lot more in red grapes. Tannins are also present in the oak barrels in which both white and red wines are aged.

If a wine is high in tannin content, it can make your mouth very dry, whereas an acidic wine is likely to make you salivate, that's a simple way to tell whether the wines you're drinking are too heavy on tannin or acid. Generally speaking, white wines are likely to be acidic, while reds will be heavy on the tannins. Perfectly balanced wines should leave the inside of your mouth neither very dry nor salivating.

These are some of the most well known red wine grapes around the world, with some tasting guidelines. Hopefully, you can find something to tempt your taste buds from this list.

CABERNET SAUVIGNON

Everyone has heard of Cabernet Sauvignon, even people who have no idea about wine at all. It's the most famous grape in the world, and there are more of them planted than anything else.

Cabernet Sauvignon is a grape that grows well almost anywhere, as long as it's not too cold, although it's most closely associated with the Medoc region of Bordeaux. These days, you're just as likely to find Cabernet Sauvignon growing in New World regions such as California, Chile, South Africa, and Argentina, as you are the Old World regions of Italy and the South of France.

Spain is now producing a lot of Cabernet wines, particularly in the Navarra region and the Penedes hills. In Spain, it's often blended with Tempranillo, and that works really well, even though both grapes are of a similar composition.

Cabernet Sauvignon is high in tannin, so it's often blended with other grapes such as Merlot or Syrah, which are less tannic. The overriding flavor is characteristically blackcurrant, and it's a full-bodied wine that is fairly high in alcohol content. It benefits from aging, as young Cabernets can be somewhat disappointing. There are a lot of potential flavors to be brought out, and they take time to develop.

MERLOT

Merlot is a good wine to help ease yourself into reds because it's low in tannin, while providing a wine that is full-bodied and high in alcohol content. It's deeply colored, and the flavors are reminiscent of plums and chocolate. You can find inexpensive Merlots, or, if the grapes come from Bordeaux's St Emilion region, you're looking at excellent quality wines, blended with Cabernet Franc. Often, Merlot is blended with Cabernet Sauvignon and Cabernet Franc to beef it up a bit.

Unlike Cabernet Sauvignon, Merlot matures more quickly, and people who find Cabernet Sauvignon difficult to deal with often enjoy Merlot. On the other hand, it improves with maturing and is unlikely to go 'off.'

Merlot's spiritual home is southwest France, and Languedoc grows a lot of Merlot grapes, producing a good quality yet inexpensive wine. It's also grown in the New World, and Californian Merlot is particularly smooth. The best Merlots are made with grapes that are very ripe and at the point they are beginning to shrivel.

SYRAH/SHIRAZ

Syrah (called Shiraz in Australia) is a grape from the Rhone Valley in France. Some experts believe Syrah grapes may have been grown in France since the Roman era, so it's a very well established grape. Syrah grapes make full-bodied wines with a fair bit of tannin, although not as much as Cabernet Sauvignon, and they are deeply colored. It really doesn't need to be blended with other grapes, but in Australia, it may be blended with Cabernet, and in the southern Rhone Valley it is sometimes paired with Grenache.

Australian Shiraz wines tend to be medium bodied and can be fruitier than French Syrahs. Flavors vary with the growing regions but are often said to taste of berries, smoked meats, and even black pepper! Probably the most well regarded Shiraz wines are those from Penfolds Grange in Australia. There are also sparkling wines around made with Shiraz grapes.

Generally, Syrah/Shiraz wines are fairly high in alcohol content and slightly sweet. Syrah wines are also being produced in Spain, Italy, and Portugal, and just about every Australian grower produces a Shiraz of some description.

TEMPRANILLO

Tempranillo is a Spanish grape and the main component of Rioja. Rioja is Spain's most famous wine, but for a long time the robust flavor of Tempranillo was disguised as Rioja, aged in American oak barrels with a vanilla scent. These days, Rioja is aged in French barrels for shorter periods, and the Tempranillo flavor takes its rightful place at center stage.

Tempranillo is also grown in Portugal, America, and Australia. You can often find a reasonably priced varietal, that is, a wine made mainly from a single grape, especially if it comes from Spain. It's a strong flavored yet mild and smooth wine, and although it's rich in tannin, it won't dry your mouth out like some wines.

You may also see Tempranillo-containing wines billed as Crianza or Ribera del Duero. It pairs well with traditional Mediterranean foods, especially anything tomato based because it has a savory flavor with it.

PINOT NOIR

Pinot Noir is the grape used in classic Burgundy wines from France. It's a grape that is seldom blended with others, because it has a distinct flavor of its own. It has a medium acidity and tannin levels, although if it's aged in oak that can increase the tannin.

Pinot Noir is the prima donna of grapes, because it's very temperamental about where it will flourish. It's picky about soil, temperature, and climate, but it's a grape well worth persevering with, as it produces some fabulous wines. It doesn't like too much heat, or too much rain, though. New World regions such as Oregon, California, Australia, New Zealand, and Chile produce some good wines from Pinot Noir. For the best in Pinot Noir, look out for the grands crus from Burgundy's Cote d'Or.

In Germany, Pinot Noir is known as Spatburgunder and produces some excellent red wines. Pinot Noir is best enjoyed young when the fruity flavors of raspberries and cherries are uppermost. It takes on a gamier flavor with age.

ZINFANDEL

Most people will identify Zinfandel as a white wine, which is actually pink, not white, just so you know. In fact, bleaching the color out of the wine, or taking the juice off the grape skins as soon as possible produces white Zinfandel. While white Zinfandel was very popular from the 1970s, and still is, to a certain extent, people are gradually realizing that red Zinfandel wine is a much superior product. That said, almost 85% of Zinfandel produced is the white variety, which is around 10% ABV.

There was some mystery surrounding the origins of the Zinfandel grape, which first appeared in California around 200 years ago. It was certainly well established by the time of the California Gold Rush in 1849, and for a long time it was thought that the grape originated there. However, recent detective work has established that it was imported into California from Croatia.

Red Zinfandel is often high in alcohol content, usually around 14%. It has fruity, spicy, and smoky flavors. It's a lighter colored wine than Cabernet or Merlot, and light bodied with a medium level of tannin that gives it a robust taste.

SANGIOVESE

The Italian grape Sangiovese is Italy's most planted grape and is the main component of Italy's most famous red wine, Chianti. These days, the proportion of Sangiovese is higher, and sometimes Chianti is 100% Sangiovese. It's high in tannin and acidity, and is usually aged in lightly oaked barrels. It ages well, with 4 – 7 years being common, although it can be aged for much longer and still improve in flavor.

As for the flavors, there are many, ranging from fruity and herby, through peppery and smoky, and several others too. Most wines made from Sangiovese grapes have characteristic cherry and tomato flavors, along with the regional variations. The reason the taste varies so much is that the Sangiovese grape takes on the characteristics of the area in which it grows, and that influences the final taste of the wine. Sangiovese grows mainly in Italy, although it also does well in Chile, Argentina, Corsica, Romania, California, and Australia.

GRENACHE/GARNACHA

Grenache is the star player in the world famous Chateauneuf-duPape, contributing approximately 75% to the finished wine. In its alter ego, Garnacha, as it's called in Spain, it's second only to Tempranillo. Most Grenache planting is in the north and east of Spain. In the phylloxera outbreak of the 19th century, it was the robust Garnacha grape that survived, and effectively saved Spain's wine industry.

Grenache is grown in France, Spain, Italy, California, and Australia, with France and Spain together growing around six times as much as the other countries combined. In France,

Grenache is particularly prominent in the Rhone Valley, Languedoc-Roussillon, and Provence.

It's a very versatile grape and wine, and it's at the heart of a number of excellent rose wines, particularly from southern France. It's thought the grape originated in Sardinia in Italy, from whence it moved to Spain and France, but this is not certain.

Grenache/Garnacha wine tastes predominantly of berries, and it can achieve high levels of alcohol, up to 15% ABV in hot countries. In fact, in some countries, wine makers are using Grenache in fortified wines such as port.

While there are many variants of red wine grapes, the ones listed above are among the most widely planted and best known grapes in the world. Because they are so well known, they also feature in some of the most famous wines. If you're new to the mysteries of viticulture and wine, it's best to start with the better known grapes and wines, because there is more written about these, and you are more likely to be able to find a wide variety of wines to try.

It's important that, as a learner in the wine game, you experience a wide range of tastes and qualities so that you can begin to educate your palate and form preferences. It's all very well and good to read wine reviews, and follow recommendations in the media and online, and indeed it's a great way to familiarize yourself with the world of wine. However, everyone's tastes are different, and a brilliant wine to one person may taste like vile plonk to another, so you really need to get a feel for the various wines out there, rather than relying on recommendations all the time. Besides, it's great fun to experiment with wine!

Before taking a look at some good wines for developing your personal preferences and building a list of favorite wines, it's a good idea to take a look at the various appellations used around the world. This will help you make your selections, and ensure you're not disappointed with the wines you choose. What's an appellation? Learn all about it in the next chapter!

CHAPTER NINE

WHAT YOU REALLY NEED TO KNOW ABOUT APPELLATIONS

Put simply, a wine appellation is the information on the label of a wine bottle that tells you where the grapes were grown that went into making the bottle of wine you're just about to open. It's protected and defined by the law of the country from which the wine originates, and it offers a measure of guarantee to the buyer, as well as protecting the growers and wine makers from unscrupulous people who may try to pass off inferior wines as Appellation Controlled.

The principle of wine appellation dates back to Biblical times, and continues through history, although it was more of a custom than a formal, legally defined structure with rules. The first legally protected growing area, the Chianti region of Tuscany, Italy, was formalized in 1716, while the first actual wine classification is credited to the Tokaj region of Budapest, Hungary in 1730.

An appellation may cover a complete region, encompassing a huge area and a large number of vineyards, or it could apply to a single, small vineyard with acreage in single figures. It really depends on the unique characteristics of a particular region, as well as the history of wine in the region.

Most countries have governing bodies or trade bureau to administer the appellations and protect the rights of the producers and the standards of the wine. Many of the most well-known French wines are appellation controlled, and indeed it was France that came up with the system on which most of the world's wine classifications are now based. The Institut National des Appellations d'Origine (INAO) was set up in 1935, as a consequence of the worldwide phylloxera outbreak in the 19th century.

Because so many vine crops were decimated, there was a lot of fraudulent practice, trying to pass off substitute grapes, and blending against tradition with grapes from other areas of France, Spain, and even North Africa. The new laws were aimed at ending poor wine making practices and restoring both quality and quantity to French wine production.

The INAO sets the geographical areas in which particular appellations may be produced, as well as determining which grapes may be grown, and in what quantities they can be harvested in a particular year, or vintage. The body also controls ripeness levels, alcoholic strength, and viticulture practices. Growers are not forced to comply with these strictures, but in order to use the local appellations, and therefore charge more for their wines, they need to follow the code rigidly.

France remained the only country implementing national wine laws until the 1970s, but then many other countries, including big producers such as Spain, Italy, Germany, Greece, Portugal, South Africa, and the South American countries began to formulate systems.

In America, the Alcohol and Tobacco Tax and Trade Bureau (TTB) regulate geographic boundaries. However, control does not encompass the vineyards. Growers can plant any grape varieties they like, and the standard and quantity of wine production is down to personal choice. Australia and New Zealand do not have an appellation system in place, although they are working towards one.

The French Appellation Controllee (AC) is not available to all vineyards and regions, and there is some protest that it's time for an overhaul to allow quality producers to display an AC on their labels. Whether that will happen is not known, and despite its strictures and restrictions, the French system remains a model for the world of wine production.

VINS DE FRANCE/TABLE WINES

So, what happens to the wines from France, and indeed other countries, which fall outside the appellation spectrum? Originally, these would be labelled as Vin de Table (table wine) in France, Vino de Mesa in Spain, simply Vino in Italy and Tafelwein in Germany.

The wines may have failed to attract an appellation for a number of reasons – grape varieties, blends, and production techniques, and until recently, these were known as table wines in all languages. It may be that you would get a varietal wine as a table wine, Merlot is a good example, but often, particularly in France, the quality of table wines was questionable. This led the INAO to introduce a new kind of classification, Vin de France, to replace Vin de Table.

The main difference is that, under the Vin de Table category, grapes could come from anywhere in the European Union. If they were exclusively French grapes, the wine would be labelled 'Vin de Table Francais.' The new category stipulates that the grapes used in Vin de France must originate in France. Germany has a similar restriction where if a producer wishes to call a wine 'Deutscher Tafelwein,' (German Table Wine), all the grapes used in the wine must be grown in Germany. Wines containing blends of grapes from across the EU must state where the grapes came from and cannot use the 'Deutscher' description on the label.

Most wine in wine boxes is table wine of one sort or another. Although it is by no means a cast iron guide, since personal tastes are so subjective, generally, the more expensive table wines will be superior to those with bargain basement prices.

VIN DE PAYS/IGP

Vin de Pays (VDP - literally 'country wine') is a step above Vin de France on the classification ladder. Europe wide, the category is known as 'Indication Geographique Protegee' (IGP). It's positioned between Vin de France (VDF) and Appellation d'Origin Controllee' (AOC).

The Vin de Pays category offers assurances to consumers, as well as allowing producers more freedom in the way they make their wines. There are three levels of VDP. The first regional level has 6 areas, while the second is based on the departments of

France. 52 of France's departments have their own VDP assigned to them. Common ones, which are likely to be well known outside France, are VDP de L'Aude and VDP de L'Herault. These can be relied on to produce quality but inexpensive red wines. Then there's the VDP de Zone tier, which is more localized, and comes nearer to AOC requirements. There are 93 of these in France.

Around 75% of all VDP wine in France is produced in the Languedoc-Rousillon area. In addition, the region is home to more than half of the VDP de Zone areas. That makes Languedoc-Rousillon the capital of VDP production in France.

In other European countries, the most important local equivalents of VDP are: Vino de la Tierra (VP, Spain), Indicazione Geografia Tipica (IGT, Italy), Vinho Regional (VR, Portugal), and Landwein (Germany, Austria).

Whether wine goes by its localized 'wine of the country' title, or the IGP protocol, or even 'IGP – Vin de Pays' or 'IGP – Vino de la Tierra,' etc., wines carrying this information on the label are likely to be of consistent good quality. You'll also pay less than for AOC wines. Table wines can be a big hit and miss, but VDP/IGP wines are pretty much guaranteed to serve up a decent wine.

It can be a bit confusing picking out a French AOC wine, because there are in excess of 300 AOC regions in France, some experts estimate there may be more than 450. Whatever the number, there are a lot of French wines to choose from. While an AOC label gives some guarantee of quality, it can still vary, depending on the vintage, because there are good years and bad years for grape harvests. We're not going to get into all that here – it's something you can pursue if you feel the need to do so, but it's not something you need to know unless you want to get heavily into vintages. If you're just looking for decent wines, the AOC or country equivalent is a good starting point.

CHAPTER TEN

SPARKLING WINES

So far, we've talked about red wines, white wines, and touched on rose wines. Sparkling wines have hardly had a mention, but now it's time to examine how they fit into the bigger picture. For many people, no celebration is complete without a glass, or several glasses, of the bubbly stuff. As a result, production of sparkling wine has increased by around 40% over the last decade. Yet it's one area of wine where possibly the most mistakes are made, because sometimes it seems almost impossible to select a sparkling wine that everyone will enjoy, and most of it gets tipped down the sink.

Mention sparkling wine and the first thing that comes to mind is champagne, but there are many incarnations of sparkling wine. Champagne comes from the Champagne region of France while sparkling wines from other regions of France are usually called Mousseaux or Cremant. In Spain, sparkling wine is generically termed Cava, while in Italy, its Spumante or Prosecco, and in Portugal it's Espumante. Sparkling wine from Germany, Austria, and the Czech Republic go by the less romantic sounding name of Sekt. Between them, France, Spain, Germany, Italy, and Russia produce around 75% of the world's sparkling wine, although Australia, South America, and the USA are now upping their production of sparkly stuff.

The sparkle in sparkling wine is carbon dioxide. This can be introduced by means of natural fermentation, which can happen in the bottle, in the traditional method, used for champagne, or in a large tank designed to stand up to pressure. The other way of introducing carbon dioxide is through injection. This pressure is the reason why sparkling wines have heavier bottles and wired corks, otherwise you'd get a shower of bubbly every time you walked past the wine rack.

Most sparkling wines tend to be white or rose, and they can vary from very dry (brut) through to sweet (doux). There are also some red sparkling wines, particularly Australian Shiraz and Italian Brachetto. So, how can you choose a really good sparkling wine that will get the party started and keep it going until the small hours? Here are a few hints.

CHAMPAGNE

Before getting into descriptions of various wines and recommendations, it's worth pointing out that no prices will be displayed here. That's because, hopefully, this book will be read all over Europe and the Americas, and maybe elsewhere too. As alcohol taxation laws vary so much, and different wine sellers have excellent offers at various times of the year, it could be misleading to quote prices for individual wines. They would very soon be out of date too, which would mean revising the book, or leaving false information in it. We will indicate if a certain wine is particularly expensive, or great value, but that's as far as it goes.

Champagne is the most famous sparkling wine of all, and true Champagne, with a capital 'C' comes only from the Champagne region of France. In fact, this region was protected long before the AOC laws came into being in 1935. The Treaty of Madrid in 1891, and then the Treaty of Versailles in 1919 gave producers in Champagne the exclusive rights to use the name. Some people won't consider any other sparkling wine but true Champagne while others think it's seriously overrated.

Champagne is almost always made from a blend of one or more of three particular grapes – Chardonnay, Pinot Meunier, and Pinot Noir. If the wine is labeled Blanc de Blancs, that means it's made entirely from white grapes, which means basically from Chardonnay. Blanc de Noirs is made exclusively from red grapes, so that's either Pinot Meunier or Pinot Noir, or a blend of the two.

The first port of call in choosing Champagne is the label. If you're looking for a dry wine, choose a 'Brut.' However, these can sometimes be a little harsh, so if you prefer your sparkles a little sweeter, go for 'Extra sec.' That might seem a bit confusing because extra sec literally means 'extra dry,' but when it comes to Champagne, it means it's still dry, but with a smoother, slightly sweeter taste. Champagne doesn't come really sweet, if you can't do dry, you're better off avoiding it altogether and going for a sparkling wine made with Moscato grapes. Brazilian wine makers in particular often use Moscato for sparkling wines, and there are some excellent qualities around.

Sticking with Champagne, though, if the label says Vintage, followed by a year of production, that means the winemaker was particularly impressed with the grapes from that particular year. Although Champagne doesn't have to be vintage to be good, it's certainly an extra marker of quality. Check with your local wine store, who can advise you on the best vintages, or of course you can research online if you feel you'd like the safety net of a vintage behind your choice of Champagne.

Some Champagne are labeled 'Reserve.' That means an older wine has been blended with the most recently produced wine to produce a non-vintage but still high-quality Champagne. The designation 'Reserve' is an indication of quality, as is 'NV Premier.' This means the winemaker didn't consider the wine to be exceptional enough to label it vintage. However, the fact that it is NV (Non-Vintage) and Premier, which is French for 'first,' means that he considers it almost good enough to be a vintage. Here are some ideas for Champagnes that will certainly not disappoint, and are on sale in most countries. Ask for more recommendations in your local liquor store.

Moet & Chandon Imperial Brut or Rose Imperial Brut is a pretty safe bet, and for a consistently high-quality Champagne, it's not ridiculously priced, and you can usually pick some up on sale. The Imperial Brut is a blend of Chardonnay, Pinot Meunier, and Pinot Noir grapes, very dry, light and lemon-scented. The Rose uses the same grape blend, but is slightly less dry, with a flavor more reminiscent of berries, with an aroma of rose petals.

Henriot Non-Vintage Blanc de Blancs has aromas of honey and orange blossom, which are echoed in the flavor of the Champagne, along with buttery tastes. It includes around 30% of reserve wines, and many wine critics consider this Champagne to be as good as, if not better than, some vintage Champagnes.

If you fancy a nice rose Champagne, try Duval-Leroy NV Prestige 1er Cru AOC Brut Rosé. Made with 90% Pinot Noir and 10% Chardonnay, both Premier Cru, it has an exotic bouquet of figs, cherries, geraniums, and ginger. You almost feel as if you've been transported to the Champagne region when you uncork the bottle. The figs and cherries are carried through in the flavors, and this is a really harmonious blend.

Champagne, like most wines, is subjective. What suits some palates may not suit others, and since decent Champagnes are rather expensive, you won't find many tastings available, unless you go to a special event. So it's a case of reading the reviews, asking for recommendations from the people who know and taking on board the kind of hints and tips that are provided in this book. It may seem like a lot of hard work just to pick a bottle of bubbly, but this is one instance where your efforts will be rewarded.

CAVA

Cava is probably the second most famous sparkling wine after Champagne. Indeed, the word cava means 'cellar' in Spanish. It was adopted fairly recently to both underline the similarities with Champagne, and also set cava out on its own as an equal player in the sparkling wine field.

However, unlike Champagne, cava has suffered from a pretty bad press over the years, due to those all-inclusive holidays and excursions in Spain that offer 'Unlimited free Cava.' The problem is, the cava they are prepared to offer for free isn't really worthy of the name, and it tends to put people off. The truth of the matter is that the best cavas are just as good as anything that comes out of the Champagne region. In fact, many people, including some of the most respected wine critics, prefer to drink a good cava rather than Champagne of similar quality. And you can buy decent cavas at a price that means you don't have to save it for special occasions. Maybe it's time for everyone to raise a glass to cava!

Cava is made using the same method as Champagne, but it's made with different grapes that are indigenous to Spain, many of which are not among the best-known grapes, so not covered in earlier chapters. Because it's made using the same method, it's probably closer in taste to Champagne than any other sparkling wine. In fact, some people refer to cava as 'The poor man's Champagne.' That's a bit of a backhanded compliment, and may have contributed to cava's bad press in some quarters.

While there is no specific region where cava is produced, which is why it doesn't merit an upper case 'C,' there are nevertheless only a few regions in Spain that produce cava.

The spiritual home of cava is in the northeast of Spain, near Barcelona in Catalonia. In particular, the area around Penedes is renowned for the quality of its cava. Cava is also produced in Rioja, Aragon, Valencia, and Badajoz, but in much smaller quantities. That's not necessarily a bad thing as some of the smaller producers can come up with excellent cavas, at competitive prices. However, 95% of all cava is produced in Catalonia, and much of that starts life in and around the Penedes region.

Codorniu is the world's oldest producer of cava, having been established in 1551. Today, it's second in production to Freixenet. These are the two most internationally recognized cava brands, and you really can't go wrong with one of them. That said, cava appreciation is subjective, as with all wines, but these trusted brands are a good place for cava virgins to make a start.

Just as with Champagne, there are three main grapes that go into cava production. They are not particularly well-known grapes and these are the top three. Macabeu is top of the list and the most important component of cava. It's a pretty nondescript grape on its own, with floral aromatics and a citrus, slightly bitter flavor. The second grape, Xarel-lo, sounds like it should be one of Superman's relatives, but it's a grape that provides heavy floral aromas, and fruity flavors to complement the Macabeu.

Paralleda, a very Spanish sounding grape, is full of acidity and abundant in citrus flavors, completing a perfect trinity of tastes and aromas.

Other grapes that may make their way into the blend are Chardonnay and Pinot Noir, which of course are two of the three Champagne grapes, along with Garnacha and Monastrell.

Generally, you won't find a sweet cava. That's just one of the ways it's such a close cousin of Champagne. Brut, again, like Champagne, is dry. Brut Nature is even drier, and very low in calories, so it's a favorite tipple for weight watchers. Semi seco has a little more sweetness, but no way could you call it sweet. If you don't do dry, go for semi seco, and if you need a little more sweetness, try a semi seco rose. Garnacha and Monastrell are added to the mix for rose cava, and Pinot Noir is beginning to make its presence felt, although it's not a typical cava grape.

These days, winemakers are starting to produce vintage cavas, and cava that is aged on the lees of the wine. In these cases, you'll find Chardonnay and Pinot Noir grapes in the blend. The vintages from 2000 to 2007 are all perceived as excellent (2000, 2006) or very good, so if you're looking for a vintage cava, check these out. When it comes to aging cavas on the lees, the figures are a minimum of 9 months for basic cavas, 15 months for Reservas, and 30 months for Gran Reservas. There are more than 270 cava producers in Spain, so in the unlikely event that Codorniu and Freixenet don't float your boat, there are plenty more to investigate.

For a great non-vintage cava, try Vega Barcelona DO (Dominacion de Origen, the Spanish Cava appellation). It's blended in almost equal quantities of the three classic cava grapes – Macabeu, Xarel-Lo, and Paralleda, and like the best cavas, its second fermentation is in the bottle. And the grapes are fermented separately before being blended, so that each is at the highest level of quality. You'll taste and smell fruits, particularly apples, pears, and citrus notes, and there's also a hint of crème brûlée there. A delicious cava can be paired with most foods and it won't break the bank either, as it's modestly priced for such excellent quality.

Another excellent cava is Freixenet Elyssia Gran Cuve Brut. In the distinctive and iconic black bottle that is the Freixenet, Elyssia is one of the newer blends. It's made using four grapes – Chardonnay (40%), Macabeu (30%), Paralleda (20%), and 10% Pinot Noir. That's an interesting combination, pairing two classic Champagne grapes with two classic cava grapes, and it works really well. It smells of honey and lemon when you open it, and its flavors are a pleasant blend of pears and apples, with lots of very bubbly bubbles. For a cava of such good quality, it's very modestly priced too. If you are new to cava, this is a good one to start with, because it does really well in bulk tastings.

Rose cava gets mixed receptions because some of the cheaper ones are only really fit to use in cocktails or sangria. Some rose cavas can have a cloying taste as a result of a little too much sweetness. However, if you want a decent rose cava, go for Codorniu's Gran Vintage Pinot Noir. Made with 100% Pinot Noir grapes, maybe that's why this particular cava is head and shoulders above most rose offerings. It has an aroma of red berries and citrus, and an attractive pale cherry color. The abundant flavor is elegant and reminiscent of strawberries.

Pinot Noir grapes can be traditionally difficult to grow, but the gravelly soils of the Catalonia region where Codorniu's estate grapes are grown hamper over production on the vine stock. The result is an excellent rose vintage cava of exceptional value, considering its quality.

Cavas can be hit and miss, particularly at the cheap end of the price spectrum. If you find yourself in Spain, experiment and try out a few, and when you find one you like, photograph the label and see if you can buy it when you get home. The ones mentioned above are certainly worth pursuing, so at least you have a heads up on cava.

PROSECCO AND SPUMANTE

Italy produces a lot of wine, in fact, it's second only to France at the time of writing (2015) and over the last ten years, it has the highest average production. So, the top three wine producers are France, Italy, and Spain in that order. How does Italy's sparkling wine compare to France and Spain? Very well, as it happens. The ones you've probably heard of are Prosecco and Spumante, with Asti Spumante being the one everyone has heard of.

Spumante simply means 'sparkling wine' in Italian, and Prosecco seems to be at the forefront of Italian sparkling wine right now. In fact, there are some stories in the media saying that supplies of Prosecco are starting to run low, but you can probably rest easy on that score. If the demand is there, the Italian wine makers will step up to the mark. In 2013, Prosecco passed Champagne in the number of bottles sold worldwide and 307 million bottles of Prosecco were sold, while Champagne could manage 'only' 304 million. So Prosecco is a bit of a modern day phenomenon, regardless of how you look at it.

Prosecco is made from Prosecco grapes, but in 2009 the grape name was formally changed to Glera. It's a grape that has been grown in Italy since Roman times, and the name had always been interchangeable, like many other grapes that have aliases. However, recently the Powers That Be decided that the name Prosecco should be reserved for wines covered by the Prosecco appellation, in the Veneto region of Italy, rather than used for the grapes that make Prosecco. It gets a little more complicated, because Prosecco/Glera isn't a single grape as there are three variations.

And there are two degrees of sparkle to Italian sparkling wines, frizzante, which is fizzy, and spumante, which is the full sparkle. So now you know. Glera is a prolific grape, ripening late season with high acidity and no overpowering flavors. That makes it ideal for sparkling wines. It's also fairly low in alcohol when made into wine, at around 8.5% ABV or slightly higher. Prosecco tends to be sweeter than Champagne or cava.

The main difference between Prosecco, Champagne, and cava is that the secondary fermentation takes place in tanks rather than the bottles. This is called the Charmat method. It's not usually aged like Champagne, so it comes with a characteristic freshness that helps those with a little knowledge to separate Prosecco from cava and Champagne in blind tastings.

The flavors of Prosecco are light and delicate featuring apples, citrus, and florals, sometimes bordering on the sweet side. And it's a more affordable drink than almost all Champagnes and many cavas. It also makes a good base for cocktails, such as the famous Venetian cocktail, Bellini. Most Proseccos are around 11% ABV.

Of the spumante sparkling wines, the most famous has to be Asti Spumante now just known as Asti after the province in Piedmont, northwest Italy. That happened in 1993, when the wine received its appellation, and it was believed that dropping the spumante suffix would lift Asti above other frizzantes and spumantes. The region is also famous for another sparkling wine, Moscato d'Asti. This is more of a frizzante and is sweeter and, at 5% - 6% ABV, lower in alcohol than Asti, which is usually around 9% ABV.

Asti is made from Moscato grapes, using a derivation of the Charmat method. It is also fermented in pressurized tanks rather than the secondary fermentation taking place within the bottle. However, the difference is that the Asti must be kept chilled, and the wine is virtually made on demand, which is a fairly unique process in wine making. The yeast is added at a later date, after the grapes have been pressed and filtered.

Avissi Prosecco DOC is an appellation wine from the Veneto, the home of Prosecco. It's fruity tasting, with a bouquet of flowers and fresh fruits. It's best drunk fairly young, and if you're wondering, the name is an echo of the sound the bubbles make as they rise in the glass. Definitely a Prosecco worth trying!

If you want a really eye-catching Prosecco for a special occasion or a gift, try Botecca Gold DOC Spumante Brut. The stylish gold bottle is designed to protect the color of the wine from the light, but it's a real talking point. The bouquet is fruity and flowery, with aromas of apples, pears, and lily of the valley. The flavor is fresh and fruity, and the bubbles foam and tickle your nose. This is a fun drink, with an elegant taste, at a very reasonable price, given its quality.

For an excellent Moscato d'Asti, try Gianmario Cerutti Moscato d'Asti Canelli (2014). It's creamy, fresh, and rather pale in color, smelling of mango, mint, and lime blossom. The flavors are delicate peaches and grapes, and a little sweetness that is light and not cloying. At just under 5% ABV, this is a light, refreshing wine that pairs excellently with desserts in particular.

Some Asti and Moscato d'Asti producers only make a small run of bottles in a particular year, so although you may find reviews for the wines, you might have a problem locating them. However, with more and more Proseccos and Astis coming onto the market each year, the choice is likely to get better and better.

OTHER SPARKLING WINES WORTH LOOKING AT

While French, Spanish, and Italian sparkling wines definitely corner the market, there are others worth considering too.

Germany, Hungary, and Austria produce some good quality sparkling wines, with Hungary coming up with sparkling wines based on Pinot Noir and Pinot Grigio grapes.

German sekt sparkling wines tend to be produced mainly from Riesling grapes, although the Pinots also make an appearance. The majority of German sparkling wine is made using the Charmat method, which means the second fermentation takes place in a pressurized tank. However, some premium sparklers are made using the traditional method used for Champagne and cava, where the second fermentation takes place in the bottle. Germany is a fairly new kid on the block as far as sparkling wine production goes as they've only been doing it since 1826.

The New World is producing some interesting sparkling wines too. Around 90% of America's sparkling wine output comes from California, and the big players in the Champagne and cava stakes have outposts there too. California is noted for a rose sparkling wine made from Zinfandel grapes using the Charmat method.

In Australia, sparkling wine production is very similar to California. Both regions have a more reliable climate for ripening grapes than the Champagne region, and again, the big players such as Moet & Chandon have outposts there. Australia is perhaps best known for its sparkling Shiraz, a wine that was first produced as 'Sparkling Burgundy' in the late 19th century. These days, it's made in the traditional way with mainly Shiraz grapes, although Cabernet Sauvignon and Merlot may figure in some blends. It's fairly high in alcohol content at around 14% ABV, semi-sweet and with a presence of tannin, so it's very different to many sparkling wines.

New Zealand is a fairly new arrival on the sparkling wine scene, having started production in the 1980s, and its pretty small scale, mostly with Chardonnay and Pinot Noir grapes. Pinot Noir, as we know, can be a bit temperamental to grow, and it's taken a while to establish a big enough crop to expand the sparkling wine industry. Look out for good things in years to come, though.

Latin America and South Africa also make sparkling wines, but at the time of writing (2015) their production is fairly small scale, and a lot of what they produce is drunk locally rather than exported. Again, it's a market worth watching for new wines in the future.

At one time, sparkling wines, particularly Champagnes, were out of the reach of most people. These days, however, modern technology and production methods, coupled with higher average disposable income, have brought these excellent wines within the compass of pretty much everyone in the developed world. Expect to see more new sparkling wines making their debuts as producers all over the world expand to keep up with the increasing demand for the sparkly stuff.

CHAPTER ELEVEN

FORTIFIED WINES

Fortified wine is any wine to which extra alcohol, usually spirits, and usually brandy, has been added. Back in the day, wine would be fortified to preserve the flavor and to prevent it from going off and developing a 'vinegar' taste. Fortification stops fermentation by killing the yeast, leaving a sweeter wine with higher alcohol content than normal.

The most common fortified wines are Sherry, Port, Madeira Wine and Marsala. There is a significant difference between spirits made from wine and fortified wines. Spirits made from wine are distilled, and reach much higher alcohol content, typically 37.5% to 40% ABV, and sometimes more for premium spirits. Fortified wines are commonly 18% - 20% ABV, and may be called dessert wines in some countries, or liqueur wines in Europe.

If the extra alcohol is added after fermentation, once the natural grape sugar has been turned into alcohol, the wine will be rather dry, as seen in many Sherries. However, adding alcohol during fermentation stops the action of the yeast and leaves natural, unfermented sugars in the wine, as in the case of Port. Now it's time to take a look at the most popular types of fortified wine, to see how they are made, and how you can choose the right one for your palate.

SHERRY

Sherry is made from white grapes, usually Palomino, which accounts for around 95% of sherry production. However, Pedro Ximenez grapes are used to make particularly prized, sweet Sherries, which the Spanish drink on special occasions. Moscatel de Alejandria grapes are also used in sherry production.

The spiritual home of sherry, which is now protected by law, is the area around Jerez de la Frontera in Andalucia, southwest Spain. The coastal towns of Sanlucar de Barrameda and Puerto de Santa Maria form what is known as 'The Sherry Triangle' with Jerez de la Frontera, and all true sherry comes from this region. The name arises from an English corruption of 'Jerez.' Sherry is the result of a harmonious blend of four main factors: climate, soil, grape types, and production techniques.

Andalucia is hot in the summer, with temperatures of 40 degrees Centigrade or more. The chalky, white, clay soil called albariza reflects the sun back up at the vines and also holds in the moisture, which is important in the searing heat of the Andalucian summer. The Barros soil that is found in the foothills and valleys is also composed of mainly clay, and the arenas, sandy soils found by the coast, are also perfectly suited to the grapes that are grown in the region.

The region experiences an average 300 days of sunshine each year, which is perfect for ripening the grapes, while the cool coastal breezes maintain acidity in the grapes and naturally cool the wine cellars.

Sherry is fermented in 600-liter American oak casks, called butts. They are only filled with around 500 liters, and a film, called a flor, forms on the surface from the yeasts. This protects the wine from oxidation, and also imparts a distinctive flavor to the sherry. After fermentation, the wines are fortified with alcohol. The finest, lightest wines are used for Fino Sherry, while the slightly darker, heavier wines are destined for Oloroso. Fino is usually fortified to 15% ABV, while Oloroso may be 17% or 18% ABV. This kills the flor and is the reason why Oloroso is often much darker than Fino, since it has no protection from the oxygen in the atmosphere.

Aside from the flor, the other thing that marks sherry out from regular wine production is the solera system, whereby the wine travels through a system of butts on different levels during maturation, each holding wines of different ages. The first level, confusingly enough, is also called a solera, and this holds the wine ready for bottling. Typically, around 10% - 15% of this will be removed, then replaced with wine from the next level, which is called the first criadera. This is a slightly younger wine, and each criadera – or level, or layer, or tier – gets slightly younger. When the wine from the final criadera is extracted, it's topped up with new wine called sobretabla. And so the process continues.

If you haven't already worked it out, this means that each batch of sherry is made from a number of different vintages, depending on the level of production. Some soleras can have a number of different layers, but three or four is typical. The solera system allows for consistency and for a house style of sherry to develop. It's exceedingly rare to come across a single vintage sherry that has not been through the solera system, although it can happen.

There is an aging system for Sherries, whereby Sherries at least 20 years old are classed as VOS (Very Old Sherries), while those over 30 years of age are VORS (Very Old Rare Sherries). Vintage Sherries from a single year are called Anadas.

The main types of sherry are:

Fino – Crisp, fresh, dry, nutty flavored and lightly colored. Fino is the closest sherry to wine, and should be served chilled and treated like regular white wine once opened. Typically 15% ABV.

Manzanilla – Protected by Dominacion d'Origen, and only produced in Sanlucar de Barrameda. The humidity in the cellars produces a thicker flor, resulting in a slightly lighter and fresher sherry than Fino, with a salty taste.

Amontillado – Aged for longer than Fino, and the loss of the flor means it develops with oxidation. It's a rich amber shade, with a nutty, more complex taste. Fortified to around 17.5% ABV, Amontillado will last for longer than Fino once opened.

Oloroso – Rich brown dry sherry that has been aged for a long time in the butt, without a flor. Nutty tasting, with a rich smell of raisins, Oloroso will keep well for some time after opening. In case you're wondering, Oloroso means 'fragrant' in Spanish!

Pedro Ximenez – The grapes for this oh-so-special sherry are air dried, then fermentation is halted with the early addition of spirit. Sweet and rather more viscous than most Sherries, it's been compared to liquid Christmas pudding by English wine critics!

Choosing a good sherry, like choosing a good wine, is somewhat subjective, but there are some guidelines to help you avoid disappointment. Don't think of sherry as something different, think of it as a DO wine local to the region, and look for the characteristics you would seek in any other wine. So, if you go for dry, light wines, you'll be happiest with a Fino or Manzanilla. If you're a red wine lover, and like something with a bit more body, an Amontillado or Oloroso may be more your scene.

Don't go for the cheapest on the shelf as that's asking for disappointment. Do a little research, look for the respected names in the industry, and read some reviews from people who know their stuff. Incidentally, did you know that Sandeman and Osborne, two highly respected sherry houses, were initially British companies? Osborne also makes some of Spain's finest brandy.

Customer reviews on online wine sellers will probably not be much help in choosing a decent sherry, because of the complexity of flavors that arises due to the production process. Another thing, too many people think of sherry as something set apart from wine, and that affects the way they approach it and review it.

Also, Sherries are at their best when paired with the right foods. Fino and savory foods are meant for one another. If you don't believe it, ask yourself why the Spanish naturally pair tapas with Fino. It's because they know their sherry, and they know their food. Ultimately though, it's all a matter of taste. If you enjoy drinking it, it's a good sherry, no matter what the reviews say.

PORT

Port is a sweet, generally red wine, often referred to as a dessert wine. It's produced exclusively in the Duoro Valley of Portugal. While some of the mass produced Ports can be of questionable quality, there are some excellent examples around, some of which will set you back a hundred dollars, or even more. Like wines, Port can also come in white and rose varieties, and there's a special, aged version called Tawny.

Remember the old way wine grapes were pressed, with workers climbing into the vats and stomping with their feet until the juice was pounded out of the grapes? Well, they still extract the juice for Port using that method. These days though, it's a mostly mechanized process with mechanical 'feet' being substituted for the real thing. Modern sensibilities probably couldn't cope with the thought of feet in their wine, and besides, it's very labor intensive. It is, however, the best way to extract juice from grapes, which is why Port producers still use a variation of the process, and some of the more renowned Port houses still use human treaders, working in unison to extract as much juice as possible from the grapes.

The soil in the Duoro Valley is called schist, it's rather rocky, but is full of nutrients and, like albariz in which Sherry grapes are grown in Andalucia, it's very good at retaining water. That's useful in the hot, dry climate of the Duoro Valley.

Unlike sparkling wines, Port is not made from a restricted group of grapes. Around thirty grape varieties can be used in port, although generally the grapes are chosen from five or six varieties that are known to produce the best wines. Touriga Nacional is the best known grape variety used in Port, and in fact it's rarely planted outside the Port producing vineyards. Touriga Francesa is more widely planted and subtler, with a high tannin level to give the Port body.

Tinta Roriz, Tinta Barocca, and Tinta Cao are also widely used in port. All thrive in the hot, dry conditions of the Duoro Valley, and have particular characteristics that contribute to excellent quality fortified wines. Tinta Cao is one of the oldest grapes in the region, and although it has a low yield, it is a major contributor to good quality Port.

The estate where grapes for Port are grown are known as Quintas, and the major producers each have their own Quintas, although they may buy in grapes from other estates to supplement their own harvest. Some Quintas produce single vintage Ports that will carry the name of the estate on the label and sell for premium prices. Grapes ripen from late June to early October, when they are harvested. That's slightly later than most wine grapes, although picking may start in mid September.

Once around half of the natural sugar in the grapes has been converted to alcohol, fortification commences, which kills off the yeast. In the making of port, a very high quality, neutrally flavored brandy is used, and roughly 100 liters of spirit will be added to 450 liters of wine, although these proportions may vary due to a number of considerations which will be assessed by the wine maker.

The wine is then left to settle for several months before being aged in casks or vats, depending on the style of the finished Port. It is capable of being kept in wood for much longer than most wines, which allows a variety of aging processes to be used. Port is an extremely long-lived wine, and a great investment, because as vintage bottles are consumed, they become more and more rare, and thus more and more valuable.

Nobody is sure where Port originated, but the story goes that during the Napoleonic Wars, the British were looking for something similar to the rich red French wines they had been drinking but which were now off the wine list for the foreseeable future. They added brandy to the rather heavy Portuguese young wines, and came up with an acceptable alternative. There's probably more than a little traction in this, because many of the main Port producers in Portugal are English companies, with English names such as Taylor's and Sandeman's.

Ruby is the cheapest, and most basic of Ports, with a rich, warming taste. Go for a premium ruby, as cheaper ones may be harsh on the palate. Tawny Port is aged for longer than Ruby, from 3 to 40 years, in fact, since Port will withstand lengthy aging better than most wines. This gives the wine its paler color, and the length of aging will be displayed on the bottle. A 20-year-old Tawny should be accessible both in terms of taste and price. Expect a dry, nutty flavor with hints of raisins.

White Port has only been around for 80 years or so. It's aged for approximately 10 years, and is best served chilled. It's a rather dry drink which is best as an aperitif and is not easily recognizable as Port.

For something further up the scale but not vintage, go for a Single Quinta or single estate Port. This is produced when the grapes are not good enough to be declared vintage, and all the grapes in the port come from a single quinta. It's the next best thing to vintage, but without the hefty price tag, and it can continue to be aged in the bottle if you wish.

Late Bottled Vintage (LBV) Port comes from grapes from a single vineyard, but again, in a year when the harvest is not good enough to declare a vintage. It's aged for about six years before being bottled, and there's likely to be some sediment left in the bottle. LBV Ports can be surprisingly good for the price you pay.

Top of the tree, and the one to aspire to, is Vintage Port. Typically, vintages are only declared on average two years in 10, although the 1990s saw a double helping, with 1991, 1992, 1994, and 1997 all being declared vintage years. Vintage Port is cask aged for two or three years then bottled unfiltered and aged in the bottle for a further 5 – 50 years. It's necessary to decant it before drinking.

There are an infinite variety of Ports available, and like all wines, your choice will be dictated by personal taste and budget. This is one area of wine where the help of a Sommelier or wine critic is invaluable in making the right choice. The right Port is a joy to the palate, so take your time in making a selection.

Sherry and Port are the most common and most popular fortified wines, but before leaving the topic, it's useful to take a brief look at the other popular fortified wines, to round off your knowledge.

MADEIRA WINE

As you might expect, Madeira Wine is produced on the Portuguese island of Madeira, in the Atlantic Ocean. It's a volcanic island, so it's rather difficult to grow decent grapes there. The story goes that when traders bought Madeira Wines, they fortified them with alcohol to preserve them on the log sea journey. The wine was then naturally heated by the warm weather conditions, producing a distinct flavor.

The main grapes used in Madeira are Malvasia, also known as Malmsey, in which George Duke of Clarence reportedly drowned in the 15th century, Boal, Sercial, and Verdelho. These produce wines varying through dry, medium-dry, medium-sweet, and sweet. Madeira wines are aged for 5, 10, or 15 years, which determines their quality. Unaged wines are not labeled with the age, but wines over 20-years-old and also made from single grape varieties are called Frasqueira, meaning vintage.

MARSALA WINE

Marsala hails from Sicily and is a famous fortified wine. It shares similarities with Madeira but is not generally so highly regarded.

Indeed, it's often seen as just a cooking wine, which is a great pity, as there are some excellent Marsalas around. It's more fruity, with flavors of apricot and vanilla predominating. Traditionally made with Grillo and Inzolia grapes, which are indigenous to Sicily, some makers have switched to the more prolific Catarratto grape, and there are seven other varieties that are used for modern Marsala.

The wines are categorized according to age. Year old wines are called Fine, at two years they are Superiore, four-year-old wine is Superiore Riserva, and five-year-old is Vergine/Soleras. 10-year-old Marsala is called Vergine/Solera Stravecchio. Colors are Oro (gold), Ambra (amber), and Rubino (ruby red), and range from dry through sweet. While Marsala has staged something of a slow recovery in the last 30 years, it still has a way to go, and may never achieve its former glories.

Whatever kind of fortified wine you go for, familiarize yourself with the production methods and levels of dryness and sweetness, as well as checking out how they are aged and for how long. And of course, as always, ask local experts and check out trusted reviews. That way you'll end up with a fortified wine to suit your palate and your budget, and there is less risk of disappointment.

CHAPTER TWELVE

GUIDE TO SERVING TEMPERATURES

When you throw a dinner party, the success of it isn't just about your mix of guests and the food you serve, it's also about how your wine is served. Far too many people pour their wines at the incorrect temperature, some even pour into plastic cups, and that is guaranteed to destroy the flavor. So, if you want to be a true wine expert, you need to know how to serve your wine, and one of the most important things is the temperature. I have also provided you with tips on glassware to use, but I will be covering this in more detail later on.

SPARKLING WINES
Sparkling wines benefit hugely from being chilled, and the ideal temperature is between 41 and 45° F. This helps to preserve the

effervescence and bring out the acidity and citrus notes. If your champagne is vintage, the temperature should be a little higher, 45 to 50° F, to bring out the biscuit and toast notes. Sparkling wines should be chilled in the fridge for up to 2 hours before you serve them.

GLASSWARE TIP

A proper champagne glass is a tall, thin flute, which is designed specifically to highlight the bouquet, concentrate the textures and preserve the wine's effervescence. You may also use a white wine glass, which is stemmed with a bowl, to allow the wine to breathe and magnify the aromas.

LIGHT DRY WHITE WINES

A tip here is to look at the color of the wine. The lighter it is, both in style and color, the colder the wine should be. As a general rule, the temperature should be between 45 and 49° F. These wines should be chilled for one and a half hours before serving.

GLASSWARE TIP

The best type of glass is a U-shaped bowl on a stem, as this will capture the fruity and floral aromas of the wine and distribute them. The rim of the glass helps to direct the wine to the front of your palate, and this balances out the fruit and acidity. The smaller glass opening also helps the wine to stay cooler for longer.

ROSÉS

These wines are best served a little warmer, at between 48 and 53° F. This is so that the complexity of their mild tannins and fruity flavors can be properly exhibited. Rosé wines come from a range of different varieties, and each has its own characteristics. As such, we apply the same rule for these as we do to the light dry wines: the lighter it is, the more it should be chilled. These should be chilled for up to one and a half hours before serving.

GLASSWARE TIP

Use a stemmed glass that has a slightly tapered bowl for a mature and full-bodied rosé. For a younger and sweeter wine, the glass would benefit from having a slightly flared lip. It is the lip of the glass that directs the flavor of the wine to the tongue, which is where the taste buds are the most sensitive.

FULL-BODIED WHITE WINES

These can be very complex wines and are best chilled to between 50 and 55° F. Take note of the taste, if it is a highly oaky wine, it should be nearer to 55, and less oaky wines should be closer to 50° F. These are best served after one hour of chilling.

GLASSWARE TIP

Think about using a classic Chardonnay glass, one that is stemmed with a round bowl and a wider rim. A glass with a wider bowl will direct the flavors and acidity to the sides and to the back of the tongue.

LIGHT TO MEDIUM REDS

These reds are vibrant and flavorful and are best served at a temperature of 54 to 60° F. If it is too warm, the fruity flavors will be acidic and tart and can be very overpowering. They are best chilled for 45 to 60 minutes before serving.

GLASSWARE TIP

Use a stemmed glass with a light taper to the rim. This will accentuate the wines that are light and fruity while the more complex wines are best served in a wider bowled glass.

FULL-BODIED RED WINES

There is a common misconception with these wines as many people believe that they should be served warm, at around 70° F, so that the alcohol dominates the flavor. The correct temperature is between 60 and 65° F, to allow the acidity and tannins to be balanced out, providing a lush flavor. These are best chilled for around 25 minutes before serving.

GLASSWARE TIP

The big and bold wines need a glass to match so make it a wide-bowled glass. The bigger surface area lets the acidity, fruit, and oaky characteristics to breathe properly, balancing everything out for a full flavor.

FORTIFIED WINES

Once again, the lighter the wine is in both style and flavor, the cooler it should be. A delicate port and a fino sherry should be served at 57 to 60° F while a vintage port or Madeira should be warmer, at around 66° F. Lighter wines should be chilled for up to 45 minutes while the darker ones should be chilled for around 20 minutes before serving.

Glassware tip – Fortified wines tend to have more alcohol in them so go with a shorter stemmed glass with a small bowl. The narrow opening will dull down the alcohol while pushing the sweetness to the front.

THINGS TO KEEP IN MIND

The time needed for chilling before serving is dependent on the starting temperature. If your wines are stored at room temperature, or around 72° F, then the above chilling times apply. If you keep them in a wine cellar or a wine refrigerator (not as cold as a standard one) then white and red wines should be chilled for 30 minutes. You can then serve your white wines immediately while the reds should be allowed to breathe for a further 30 minutes, at room temperature, before you serve them.

If your wines have been rested on a rack, use a wine bucket that has been filled with ice and water in equal amounts to chill the wines – 20 minutes for white wines and 10 minutes for reds before serving. If you are choosing a young red that is highly tannic or an old vintage, decant it 30 minutes before serving. In the young wine, the tannins will become softer, and the background characteristics will come through while, in a vintage wine, the flavor will open and become well balanced. This might sound stupid, but there really is a right way to open a bottle of wine. Before you learn how, you will need one good piece of equipment – a decent corkscrew. It does not need to be anything fancy or expensive; it just needs to have a serrated blade on it to make it easier to cut the foil.

So, if you are ready, let's get that bottle open!

1. Hold the wine bottle still

2. Using the serrated blade cut the foil across the top, front, and back. Do be sure to keep your fingers clear of the blade and of the foil, which will cut you just as easily as the knife

3. Set the corkscrew just off the center of the cork and insert it, rotating it straight down into the cork

4. Continue until there is just one curl left on the corkscrew

5. Lever it on the first step, followed by the second and then ease the cork out with your hand.

CHAPTER THIRTEEN

HOW TO BECOME A WINE CONNOISSEUR?

If you truly have a love for wine and an incredible interest in everything related to it, you might as well work towards becoming a real connoisseur. Take a look at the basic steps that you need to go through to attain this title.

- Firstly, try to get as much knowledge about wine as you can. The foremost step has to be to learn how to drink it properly. You first need to "see" the wine. Look at the color to determine the age of the wine. A white wine is darker with age while red wines get lighter as they age. The next step is to "swirl" it. Hold the glass and swirl the wine around the glass in gentle motions so that it coats the sides. This will cause the aroma of the wine to release. You then need to "smell" the wine. In a white wine, you will usually detect citrus notes or vanilla. In red wines, berry scents or darker plum scents are more evident. Now you can finally "sip" the wine. This helps you evaluate both the taste and the smell of the wine.

- You need to know about tannins as well as terroir properly. Tannins will help you understand the texture of the wine while terroir is all about where the wine was grown. Terroir refers to the climate, soil, etc. of the place where the wine was grown.

- Learn about the correct serving temperatures of each wine as they differ. For instance, the temperature should be below 5 degrees Celsius or 59 degrees Fahrenheit when it comes to sparkling wines or white wines. In case of red wine, the appropriate temperature varies from 20 to 25 degrees.

- The glass in which the wine is served is also important. The glass itself will also help in adding to the experience of the wine. Certain shapes and sizes of glasses are better suited to certain wines. For instance, you will notice how flutes are often used for serving vintage sparkling wines. You should then know how to hold this glass properly and drink the wine in the correct manner.

- Get to know as much of the wine glossary as you can. This will help you in describing the wine you are drinking.

This is the most basic thing that a wine connoisseur needs to be able to do. The main point of it is to accurately describe exactly what is on your palette.

- Cultivate your taste of wines. Try out as many wines as you can and study them as you drink. Experience is the best teacher. Go to wine tastings, and ask for recommendations from shops and other connoisseurs. This will all help to hone your wine tasting abilities. Go around wineries to get a proper sense of how the wine is made and to learn how that wine should be consumed. Joining wine groups is yet another trend that has grown over time. Spending time with others who have a similar love for wine will work to your benefit.

- Develop your palette. Start branching out and try out as many types of wine as you can. You won't know exactly what type of wine suits you until you try it out. Becoming a connoisseur is about knowing more about wine than others. It is not just about drinking the one wine that you liked. You will soon acquire a taste for having the right wine with the right food or at the right occasion.

- Always spend time finding out more and more about wine so that you can be called a true wine connoisseur.

- You need to start talking confidently about all the wines that you drink and describe them in terms that are more than just average adjectives. You should be able to identify the aromas, components, age, etc. of the wine when you drink them. You should make an effort to know more about the grape varieties as well as different regions where all the wine comes from.

- As you build up your wine knowledge and expertise, you can also choose to go a step further and get a certificate. You can sit for tests or even take up a course to become a professional wine sommelier.

TERMS USED TO DESCRIBE WINES OR WINE TERMS:

The world of wine is one on its own and knowing certain words will help you stand firmer in it. These terms and the many more associated with wines will help you understand the exact descriptions of wines while they are being evaluated. You also learn more words related to anything that has to do with the production, taste, manufacture, etc. of wine.

- Fleshy - this means that the acidity level is low and flavors are more concentrated in the wine.
- Hard - this means that the wine has astringent tannins.
- Forward - this means that the wine is ready for being consumed early.

- Rich - this means that the wine has a high concentration of the ripe fruit.
- Full-bodied - this means that the wine has a high concentration of both fruit and alcohol.
- Soft - this means that the wine is fruity but has acidic balance as well.
- Tannic - this means that the wine has a firmness that gives it more potential for aging well.
- Blanc - used to describe white wines.
- Blind tasting - this means that you have to taste and discover the wine without knowing its name.
- Cantina - this means winery in Italian.
- Length - this refers to how long you can taste the wine in your mouth after you have swallowed it. The longer you can feel the taste, the better is the quality of the wine.
- Viscous - this means that the wine is thick and concentrated with a lot of fruit extract as well as glycerine.
- Chiaretto - this means pale color rose in Italian.
- Dessert wine - this means the wine is quite sweet and has low alcohol as long as it is above 15%.
- Acescence - this means that the wine has a sharp and tangy flavor that might be accompanied with the smell of vinegar.

- Aperitif - this means that the wine is drunk without food or before a meal so that the appetite is stimulated.
- Aging barrel - these are used for aging wines and are usually made of oak.
- Altar wine - this is a type of wine used for Catholic Church ceremonies.
- Astringency - this means or refers to how much tannin is there in the wine and how much it makes your mouth pucker after drinking.
- Aromatic - this means that the wine has very distinctive aromas.
- Tightly knit - this means that the wine is young, highly acidic and has tannin. It is still not open and done.
- Balanced - this means that the elements of the wine are all balanced and there is not any one component that dominates the others.
- Baume - this is the measure of how much sugar is in the wine.
- Body - this refers to how the wine feels in your mouth. A thin wine will have a light body such that it is not too heavy but has full flavor. A thick wine will have a robust quality.
- Claret - this means that the wine is Bordeaux wine and is a British term.

- Crackling - this means that the wine is slightly effervescent.
- Demi-sec - this means that the wine has moderate or medium levels of sweetness.
- Dry - this means that the wine has extremely low or zero residual sugar level.
- Extra dry - this means that there is just a little residual sugar.
- Flabby - this means that the wine has low acidity and lacks structure.
- Hard - this means that the wine is unpleasant due to excessive tannin.
- Mulled - this means that the wine has been spiced and heated.
- Reserve - this means that the quality of the wine is higher than usual.
- Still - this means that the wine is not of the sparkling variety.
- Tart - this means that the level of acidity in the wine is high as in younger wines. Young - this means that the wine is not matured.

CHAPTER FOURTEEN

THE RIGHT GLASS FOR THE RIGHT WINE

It doesn't matter whether you are drinking a sweet or dry wine, a light, medium, or full-bodied wine, or a red or white. The right glass for the right wine will bring out the best, in flavor and aroma, of your favorite wine. Understanding which glass is right for each wine and why one glass is better than another is essential if you want to get the best out of your wine and become a true connoisseur.

THE DIFFERENT PARTS OF A WINE GLASS

THE FOOT
This is what allows the glass to stand upright.

THE STEM

This lets you hold your glass without transferring heat from your hands to the wine, thus warming it up and without leaving greasy smudges on the glass. Believe it or not, dirty glasses detract immensely from your visual enjoyment and this affects the way you taste your wine.

THE BOWL

This part of the glass serves a number of different purposes, and there is quite a wide variation in bowls. All wine glass bowls are tapered up, and the opening is wider than the base of the bowl, although not by much in some cases. The shape helps to capture the aroma and distribute it evenly towards the nose and mouth.

Wine glass bowls are also designed with the surface area in mind - red wine glasses have a bigger surface area so that the wine can breathe, while a white wine glass has a smaller area. Champagne glasses are smaller still so that wine can retain the carbonation, or effervescence.

THE RIM

This is vital for achieving the best experience. Thin rims cause less distraction from the wine. Good glasses have "cut" rims that are smooth and do not stop the wine from flowing smoothly.

Cheap glassware tends to have thick and bumpy rims that, although they are still practical, may distract from the wine.

THE COLOR

The very best wine glasses are clear, crystal clear to be frank, and this allows the wine's beauty and subtle nuances to shine through. You can use colored glasses as they will not detract from the taste but clear glasses are the best if you want to display your wine to its best.

WHICH IS BEST – CRYSTAL OR GLASS

A wine glass tends to be made from glass or crystal, but is there any real difference? Obviously, crystal is glass but the reverse is not true, not all glass is crystal. What determines the classification of glass or crystal is the lead content. Lead softens the glass in a crystal glass, making it easier to cut and engrave. It also makes the glass heavier and allows for diffraction of the light. Traditional glasses are much lighter and do not diffract light.

In traditional lead crystal glass, the lead would leach out and, to stop this from happening, modern crystal glassware does not contain lead. Instead, a combination of barium carbonate, titanium oxide, and zinc oxide are used. This ends up producing a glass that has similar features to lead crystal, such as the ability to control temperature and to bring out the flavor and aroma of your chosen wine. They also have the refractive property of lead crystal but are not so heavy in weight.

It is widely thought that the highest of quality crystal glasses do make your wine taste better, but the high cost of them prevents many people from being able to afford them. They are also extremely fragile, making them much more expensive to replace than an ordinary plain glass. In all fairness, whether you choose to go with crystal or glass, your wines will benefit from being served in the right type of glass, which is what I am going to talk about next.

RED WINE

Fermenting red or black grapes in their skins produces red wines, the skin is what gives you the red color to your wine. Red wines tend to have a strong flavor and pair with similar meals, such as red meats, and pasta dishes, etc.

The right glass for red wine is a large glass. It should have a round, full bowl with a large opening, bigger than any other glass of a similar size, as this allows the wine to breathe. This also allows you to get your nose in the glass to detect the aroma.

The style of the bowl is vital because red wines have a complex nature, or flavors and aromas and need a large surface area to ensure they come into contact with the air.

Examples of red wine glasses include the Bordeaux glass, which tends to be taller than a normal red wine glass but also has a smaller bowl. It is ideal for the fuller bodied and richer red wines like Merlot or Cabernet. The tall nature of the glass lets the wines go directly to the back of the mouth so that the flavor is maximized.

Another popular red wine glass is the Burgundy glass, which is designed for the lighter, full-bodied wines, like the Pinot Noir. It isn't as tall as a Bordeaux glass but it does have a much larger bowl, which directs the wine to the tongue, maximizing the delicate flavors.

WHITE WINE

White wines are made from black or white grapes that have the skin removed before they are fermented. They are often combined with spicy and citrus flavors. White wines tend to be enjoyed colder than red and are best served with fish or poultry dishes.

A white wine glass tends to be more U-shaped and stand more upright than a red wine glass. This allows the aroma of the wine to be released while keeping the temperature cooler. The best glass style for a young white wine will have a bigger opening to allow the taste to be directed to the sides and the tip of the tongue, bringing out the sweetness. More mature white wines prefer taller and straighter glasses so that the wine is directed to the sides and back of the tongue, enhancing the bolder flavors.

SPARKLING WINE

Champagne and sparkling wines give off a hint of luxury through their texture of bubbles and fizz. The sparkles in the sparkling wine are carbon dioxide bubbles, a by-product of the process of fermenting.

The right glass for a sparkling wine is a tall upright glass that is narrower than most other wine glasses. The reason for this is to retain the sparkle and keep the flavor of the wine intact.

ROSE WINE

Rose wines tend be to blush or pink in color and this coloring comes from the skin of the grape. This is included in the fermentation process for just the first few hours. Sometimes the color comes from the fact that red and white wines are mixed together. Most of these are medium to sweet in taste although those from European climates can be quite dry.

There are two types of glasses that you can use for Rose wines, those with a short bowl that is slightly tapered on a stem and those that have a flared lip to them. You can also get away with using a white wine glass because the fermentation process for both types of wine is similar.

Younger wines that are somewhat crisper and less sweet will prefer a slightly flared lip to the glass. The flared lip allows the wine to run out of the bowl and directs it to the tip of the tongue. Because the taste buds are more sensitive here, the sweetness is enhanced, allowing crisper wines to taste more balanced and removing some of the bite.

The more mature Rose wines should use the glass with a slight taper. The bowl is short and rounded, similar to the other glasses, but is shaped somewhat more tapered and shorter than a traditional red wine glass.

DESSERT AND FORTIFIED WINES

Dessert wines are sweet and are usually served with a dessert, as the name implies. There are many different types of dessert wine and as such, a general rule should be that it is sweeter in taste than the dessert it is being served with.

Fortified wine is made from ordinary wine that has had liquor blended in. This is usually brandy, which is nothing more than wine that has been distilled. This gives the fortified wine a distinctive flavor and an alcohol content that is higher than normal wine.

Glasses for these types of wine should be smaller so that the wine is sent to the back of the mouth; this stops the sweet nature of the wine from overwhelming the other flavors. Because the wine tends to be higher in alcohol, a smaller wine glass is recommended, for smaller servings.

SPECIALTY GLASSES
Add section on specialty glasses or remove.

ALL-PURPOSE
If you can only afford to purchase one type of glass, you should consider an all-purpose wine glass. The experience will not be quite the same as it would be through the correct glass, but they do offer a function that is similar as well as being cheaper and more efficient. The shape of the bowl is somewhere between that of a white wine glass and a red wine glass, making it perfectly acceptable to use it for either type of wine.

STEMLESS WINE GLASSES

Stemless wine glasses offer the same range of shape and styles that traditional wine glasses offer and deliver complete functionality with a more modern style and are less prone to breaking as well. Wines will warm up quicker than a traditional stemmed glass because the glass is in constant contact with your hand. However, the design is contemporary and are all the rage right now, and that may well be worth the risk of warmer wine. As well as that, because they don't have delicate stems, they don't need such delicate handling to preserve them.

CHAPTER FIFTEEN

LEARN HOW TO TASTE WINE LIKE AN EXPERT

Liking the taste of a particular wine is all well and good but do you know why you like the taste? Professional wine tasters can describe a wine, right down to its individual components. If you want to learn how to taste wine and evaluate it the way an expert does, read on for more tips.

THE RIGHT TASTING CONDITIONS

The very first thing you need to do is make sure that your tasting conditions are right. Take note of everything about your circumstances that could affect the way your wine tastes. For example, is the area noisy? Are there a lot of people there? This can make it difficult to concentrate. What about the smells in the room, are there a mix of perfumes, cooking smells, even pet smells? These can all work towards destroying your ability to be able to clearly determine the aromas in the wine. If the glass is too small, too big, too tall or too short, not the right shape or smelling of detergent, this can also affect the flavor of the wine.

What temperature is the wine? Is it too warm or too cold? This will have an impact on your first impressions, as will the age and any flavors that may be left over from what you previously ate or drank.

You need as near to neutral conditions as you can possibly get for wine tasting so that the wine is able to stand on its own and is not affected by any external influences. If the wine is too cold, you can warm it up by cupping your hands around the bowl. If the glass appears to be somewhat musty, rinse it with wine, NOT with water, making sure you swirl it around to cover the entire bowl, this is known as glass conditioning. Lastly, if there are any strong aromas around, perfume in particular, walk away and try to find neutral air.

EVALUATING BY SIGHT

Once you have gotten your tasting conditions as neutral as you can, it's time to take a look at the wine that is in your glass. The glass should be around a third full to get the best experience. Follow these steps to perform a visual evaluation of the wine:

Straight angle – look down into the glass, then hold the glass up into the light before tilting it so that the wine rolls to the edges of the glass. This lets you see the entire range of colors in a wine, not just the central darkness.

When you look down into a glass of wine, you can get a real sense of the color depth, and this will offer up clues to the density and the saturation. As you become experienced, you will learn to identify particular varieties of grapes by the scent and the color of the wine. For example, a wine that is a deep saturated black or purple color may be a Syrah or a Zinfandel, while a lighter shade, more pale, could be a Pinot Noir or a Sangiovese.

Holding the glass to the light and looking at the wine through the side of the glass can show you how clear the wine is. Murky wines may have issues with chemicals or with the fermentation process. Or, it could just be that the wine has not been filtered or contains a little sediment because it was shaken before being poured. The best sign is wine that is clear and brilliant and has a little sparkle to it.

Tilting the glass allows the wine to thin out, and that can give you an idea of the weight and the age of it. If the wine is pale and watery towards the rim, it suggests that the wine may be rather insipid and thin. If it is a brown or tawny color in a white wine or an orange/rusty red in a red wine, it indicates that the wine is older, or it has been oxidized and is most likely past its best.

SWIRL

The last step is to give the wine a good swirl. Keeping the glass on a flat surface, for beginners, is easier to accomplish this as it is not recommended to swirl the glass in the open-air freestyle manner that you see experts doing. Watch to see if the any legs or tears run down the side of the glass. Wine that has good legs has a higher content of alcohol and glycerin and this tends to indicate a bigger denser wine.

THE SNIFF TEST

So, you've given the wine a good visual look, and now it's time to sniff it. Swirl the glass but do not dip your nose right into it. Instead, hover your nose over the top of the glass, take a number of short quick sniffs, and then move away from the glass. Now the information needs to filter through to your brain.

There are lots of different guides that you can use to help you train your nose in identifying the key aromas in the wine; some of these guides are good, and some are bad. There are thousands of different aromas and a single glass may contain many of them so don't worry about identifying all of them. Yes, it can be fun to try to name all the different fruity, herby, spicy, and floral smells in a single glass of wine but it is time consuming and it certainly is not essential. Instead, once you have taken those few short sniffs, try to identify the following key aromas, these will help you to understand the characteristic of the particular wine you are sniffing.

FLAWS

First, let's just take a look at some of the flaws that you may come across, indicators that a wine has spoiled. A corked wine will give off a musty aroma, similar to that of an old attic and may have the taste of wet newspaper. This is a flaw that cannot be fixed.

A wine that has a strong dose of SO2 included in the bottling process will give off a smell not dissimilar to burnt matches but this will disappear with a little vigorous swirling.

A vinegary smell indicates volatile acidity while a smell of nail polish indicates the presence of ethyl acetate. Brettanomyces is a yeast that is certainly not desirable in wine, and it smells strongly of sweaty saddles. A little of this "Brett" can give a red wine an earthy component, but too much of it will work to obliterate the fruit flavors.

Learning how to identify the most common flaws in wine is just as important as being able to identify the individual components that make up the wine. It will also help you in understanding yourself, your own blind spots and palate sensitivities, and these are key to learning how to choose a wine that you will enjoy.

FRUIT AROMAS

If no particular aroma jumps out at you, concentrate on the fruit. Wine, as you know, is made from fermented grapes so you should get an aroma of fresh fruit, unless the wine is very cold, old, or very sweet.

You can learn to identify specific fruits and grape varieties. Many grapes will offer up a spectrum of different fruit scents that you can use to identify the condition the grapes were grown in.

FLOWERS, LEAVES, HERBS, SPICES, & VEGETABLES

You will find floral aromas are more common in wines made with cool-climate grapes, like Riesling and in some of the Rhône varieties, like Viognier.

Some grapes have a grassy or an herby scent. The Sauvignon Blanc is grassy while a Cabernet Sauvignon may carry the scent of herbs and vegetation. Many tasters indicate that the best herbal aromas should be those that are delicate and not overpowering. The best wine aromas can be complex, but they are harmonious, specific, and balanced.

Another common aroma is an earthy one, somewhat like mushrooms, leather, damp earth, and rock, and these tend to exist mainly in red wines. The mushroom smell can help you to identify a region, but too much of mushroom smell could just be an indication that the grapes did not ripen properly or were from an inferior clone.

Occasionally, in a very fine red or white, you may get scents of rock, mineral, or earth. This indicates the conditions of the vineyard that come across as specific flavors and scents in the finished wine.

WINE BARREL AROMAS

If you can smell smoke, toast, chocolate, vanilla, caramel, or even roasted nuts in the wine, you are most likely sniffing a wine that has been aged in a new oak barrel. There are a number of factors that affect this, including the age of the barrel, the type of oak used, the char level, the way the barrel was made and how the winemaker has chosen to mix and match the different factors, these all have an impact on the different flavors and scents that are evident in finished wine.

Secondary Aromas

A young white wine and a young sparkling wine may smell something like beer and this is because of the yeast that was used. Some dessert wines have a smell of honey and are typical of some of the best Sauternes. Chardonnays that have a smell of caramel or buttered popcorn have more than likely been cycled through a secondary fermentation process. Known as a malolactic process, it converts the malic in the wine to lactic acid, which tends to soften the wine and enhance the aromas. Older wines don't tend to have such fruity aromas but are more complex.

The effort that goes into putting the wine aromas into words is designed to help you to focus, to understand, and to hang on to our personal impressions of a particular wine. The idea is to build up a store of different smells and what each one means. The language of wine is what adds true value to a wine tasting. Learning that language, provided you don't overdo it, can also help to get rid of some of the common wine myths, such as those that surround the descriptions on a wine label.

Evaluating by Taste

After all of that, it is now time to take your first taste of the wine. Do not be tempted to gulp, instead just take a sip. Suck on it as if you were trying to pull the wine through a straw as this aerates it and circulates it fully around your mouth.

You will come across a wide range of different floral, fruity, herby, mineral, and barrel favors, amongst others and, if you did your sniffing homework properly, you would be able to identify those that follow on from where your nose left off. Besides identifying the flavors, your taste buds are also determining whether the wine is harmonious, balanced, evolved, complex, and complete.

BALANCED

Balanced wines should exhibit a balanced proportion of the base flavors. Don't forget that our taste buds are able to identify four main flavors – salty, bitter, sweet, and sour. Sweet and sour flavors are important in wine; salty tastes are hardly ever encountered and the bitterness should not actually be a bitter taste, more of a feeling of astringency caused by the tannins.

Most dry wines tend to have a mix of flavors that are derived from the different aromas, as well as the tastes of the acids, alcohol, and tannins, these cannot be detected just by smell.

There is not one single formula for all wines, but there should be a proper balance. If a wine is too sweet, too sour, too hot in terms of alcohol, too bitter, too astringent, or has a lack of acids, it is not very well balanced. If it is a young wine, it will not age very well, and if it is a mature wine, it is past its best.

HARMONIOUS

Harmonious wines are those whose flavors are integrated seamlessly. It is perfectly possible for all of the components to be proportioned well in a wine but still stand out individually, especially in a young wine. They can be identified, but if you can feel them all, feel the edges here they have not blended well. A good young wine is one whose flavors are already together harmoniously.

COMPLEX

This can mean a number of things and the best gauge of your progress in wine tasting will be your ability to detect the complexities and appreciate them. The simplest flavors, like a strong vanilla or a ripe, jammy flavor, will remind you of soft drinks, and it is natural for a new wine taster to associate them as such to start with. Indeed, some of the more successful wines have been blended with these flavors in mind but they are not rich in complexity.

Complex wines will dance in your mouth. They will change throughout the tasting and, like a good painting, they will change the more you taste them. In an older wine, these complexities will evolve. Whether a wine is young or old, the length of it will provide an indication of its complexity. To determine this, note how long the flavors stay in your mouth after you have swallowed. Most beginners are too eager to move on to the next sip with a really good wine so try to learn restraint and patience, let the wine finish dancing before you move on.

COMPLETE

A complete wine is one that is balanced, complex, harmonious, and evolved, and has a satisfying taste that lingers. These wines deserve your full attention because they have so much to offer, more so than any other wine.

Now that you have a basic understanding of what it takes to taste wine like an expert, it's time to go off and start practicing. Build up a record of your tastings, of what you learn and what you get out of it so that you can compare notes. Make sure your notes are full and describe the characteristics of each wine, the flavors and aromas, and complete this for wines that you like and dislike.

CHAPTER SIXTEEN

GUIDELINES ON PAIRING THE RIGHT FOOD WITH THE RIGHT WINE

Believe it or not, this is important as it will ensure that you get the best experience, not just from the wine but from your food as well. Before I go into details on what wine goes with what food, I first want to tell you a few simple rules, guidelines if you like, on how to get started.

Pick a wine that you will like.

Think about the dish or the whole meal and ask yourself what its main characteristics are:

- Is it a mild dish or full of flavor?
- Is it a fatty or a lean dish?
- Is it acidic or is it rich?

Bear these characteristics in mind when you choose your wine and make sure that the wine will:

- Keep the flavors balanced. Mild foods should be matched with mild wines while dishes that are big, bold, and full of flavor should be matched with a similar type of wine. You also want to match the richness of the food to the wine

- Cleanse the palate with acids or tannins. A rich fatty meal, for example, will require a red wine that has a good level of tannins to help to cleanse your palate. If you want to match a white wine to rich fatty meals, make sure the wine contrasts the food, perhaps a crisp and acidic white. This rule can be ignored if the food is just fatty and not rich.

- Match acid with acid. Acidic meals should be accompanied by an acidic wine, one that is able to keep up with the level of acids in the meal.

Keep in mind that acidic wines do not match well with a creamy dish and will usually cause a nasty clash.

If you are eating a food that contains strong spices, bear in mind that those spices can destroy the taste of a wine so try and avoid wine if you can with these meals. If you have to drink wine, go for a spicy and sweet wine, perhaps something that is a little dry.

When in doubt, remember that a wine will generally do very well with a food that it grew up with so pair Italian foods with Italian wines, German with German, French with French, etc. It isn't a true requirement but it can help to simplify things.

Simple guidelines for choosing what type of food go with each kind of wine successfully:

- The flavors of the food as well as wine should be similar so that they complement each other. For example, Sauvignon Blanc should be paired with citrus food. Mild flavored wine like Muscadet would go well with oysters. The weight of the food is different from the intensity of flavor. The intensity of a heavy dish could be high if it has sauce but light if it does not. Spicy dishes go well with Gewurztraminer. Seafood is complemented with delicate wines like Pinot Grigio or Soave.

- The weight and texture of the food should also be similar to be complementary. Full bodied wines go well with rich food like meat casseroles. The weight of the wine is more important than the color. Delicate wines go with fish and such lightweight food. Chardonnay is medium weight and matches with similar food such as lobster.

- Pair salty dishes with crisp wines like Sauvignon Blanc. A hint of sweetness in the wine helps to balance out and enhances the salty food. Champagne goes well with salty appetizers served during meals.

- Tannin levels should be higher if the texture of the food is greater. The tannin content varies in different wines. High tannin wines are those such as Malbec and Cabernet Sauvignon. Lamb pairs well with tannin wines as the tannin strips the protein from the mouth and cleanses your palate.

- The level of sweetness of the wine should either be higher than or similar to the sweetness of the food. If the wine is dry and consumed with sweet food, it may taste too acidic. Foie gras is well paired with Barsac or Sauternes. Blue cheeses are well complemented with sweet wines as well.

- Certain wines pair well with certain sauces. For example, Chardonnay pairs with mushroom sauces while Sauvignon Blanc pairs with citrus sauces.

- Pair spicy food with wines with a sweet overtone. This helps to balance the palate when the food is spicy like in Asian dishes.

- The acid level of the wine should be higher than or equal to the acidity of the food you pair it with. Fatty food is complemented with wines that have high acidity. Cool climate wines have higher acidity than those from warmer places. High acid wines help in cleansing the palate when paired with oily dishes. High acid wines are needed to complement food with a lot of lemon juice or vinegar. Chianti, Valpolicella, and other such Italian red wines compliment dishes with a lot of olive oil in them.

Guide to pairing wines with food using ingredients as examples:

- Sauvignon Blanc - Pine nuts, chicken, green apples, citrus, oysters, scallops, light sauces, turkey, sorbet desserts, asparagus.
- Chardonnay - Almonds, shrimp, apple, potato, chicken, veal, sweet or barbecue sauces, ginger seasoning, squash, mango.
- Pinot Noir - Walnuts, Brie, clove, nutmeg, mushrooms, red sauce, white chocolate desserts, figs, tuna, roast chicken, lamb, and strawberries.
- Malbec - Shark, rosemary, Cajun sauce, barbecue sauce, chocolate, blueberries, baked potato dishes, duck meat, burgers, pork ribs.
- Merlot - Chestnuts, tuna, swordfish, mint, rosemary, Bolognese sauce, dark chocolate, onions, steak, grilled meat.

- Cabernet Sauvignon - Tuna, walnuts, cheddar cheese, lavender, rosemary, tomato sauce, gelato, broccoli, tomatoes, venison, beef.

- Zinfandel - Ripe brie, eggplant, pork, duck, beef, Cajun sauce, salsa, gingerbread, nutmeg, cranberries, blackened fish.

- Gewürztraminer - Pork, Chinese food, salmon, Thai cuisine, spicy dishes, peppered cheese.

- Petit Syrah - Tuna, salmon, duck, quail, cheddar cheese, thyme, basil, bay leaf, lamb.

- Rose - Salmon, pork, ham, goat cheese, Gouda, basil, chives, curry seasoning, chicken, sea bass, trout.

- Chianti - Tomato, game, lamb, duck, beef, strong cheese.

- Brut: Dry - Cream sauce, shellfish, sole, mild cheese.

- Chenin Blanc - Fruit desserts, cream sauce, shellfish, sole, poultry, spicy dishes, pork, mild cheese.

- Riesling - Creamy desserts, cream sauce, fruit desserts, shellfish, poultry, spicy food, pork, mild cheese.

- Tempranillo - Tomatoes, game, lamb, duck, beef, strong cheese.

- Torrontes – Mozzarella cheese, grilled chicken, pineapple, sushi, mango, sea bass, garlic, basil, peanut sauce, cheesecakes, smoked meat.

BASIC TIPS FOR PAIRING WINES DURING MEALS:

CHAMPAGNE

Salty foods are quite well paired when served with dry sparkling wines such as Spanish cava or brut champagne. This is because they have a certain sweetness that complements the salty foods.

SAUVIGNON BLANC

Sauvignon Blanc is a zippy type of wine that goes well with tangy food items like sauces and dressings.

GRUNER VELTLINER OR VERMENTINO

These are well paired when served with food that has a lot of fresh herbs in it.

PINOT GRIGIO

Fish or any light seafood dish matches with white wines like the Pinot Grigio.

CHARDONNAYS

If the fish is fatty or cooked in rich sauce, it tastes even better with some white Chardonnays.

RIESLING

Rieslings or Vouvrays are slightly sweet and hence work well with spicy dishes like those from Indian cuisine.

ASTI SPUMANTE

This is moderately sweet and sparkling and complements desserts that have fruits quite well. The tastes of the fruit components are even more emphasized by such wines.

ROSE CHAMPAGNE

Such sparkling wines are quite well paired with main course dishes like risottos.

DRY ROSE

Dry Rose is served well with most types of cheese as it has the characters of both white and red wine that complement cheeses.

DOLCETTO AND PINOT NOIR

These light bodied wines taste good with food that has earthy ingredients like truffles or mushrooms.

SHIRAZ AND MALBEC

These wines are bold enough to be served with food containing heavy sauces. The flavor of both the dish as well as the wine does not overpower each other.

CABERNET SAUVIGNON AND BORDEAUX

These wines are a great pair with juicy meat.

CABERNET FRANC

This type of wine has a spicy tone that complements well-seasoned meat.

PAIRING WINES WITH DESSERTS:

Let us look at how some of the most common desserts can be paired with their complementary wines.

DARK CHOCOLATE

Pair this with wines like Madeira or Tawny Port that are fruity red wines that are soft and dry.

MILK CHOCOLATE

Pair this with fortified and oxidative wines that have a nutty element such as Madeira and Sweet Oloroso.

CHOCOLATE ICE CREAM

Pair this with a Muscat that is rich and sweet such as the Rutherglen Muscat.

CRÈME CARAMEL

Pair this with a Barsac or Semillon.

CUSTARD

Pair this with Muscat's or Rieslings that are sweet.

APPLE PIES OR TARTS

Pair this with some Coteaux du Layon.

FRUIT SALADS

Pair these with wine that is light and sparkly such as the Moscato d'Asti.

PAIRING WINES WITH CHEESE:

Cheese is one of the most crucial pairings with wine and getting it right is essential.

GORGONZOLA

Pair this with some Tawny Port that has aged.

CAMBOZOLA

Pair this with some sweet wine like Tokaji Aszu.

GOAT'S CHEESE

Pair this with some Pouilly Fume or Sauvignon Blanc.

CHEDDAR AND PARMESAN

Pair these with some reds that are medium or full-bodied dry wines like Red Bordeaux.

SMOKED CHEESE

Pair this with some Gewurztraminer.

BRIE

Pair this with some rich White Burgundy.

MIMOLETTE

Pair this with some Red Bordeaux.

PAIRING WINE WITH FISH:

The preparation of the fish is what determines the wine that it should be served with. The constitution of fish itself is quite light, so the ingredients of the dish are what are important.

FISH CAKES

Pair these with some white wine that is crisp such as Chablis and Pinot Grigio.

WHITEBAIT

Pair this with some dry white wine like Muscadet.

COD

Pair this with some Pinot Grigio if it is fried and some Chardonnay if it is grilled.

SOLE

Pair this with some white Bordeaux.

TUNA AND SALMON

Pair these with some white wines that are bigger like Chardonnays from Australia.

MACKEREL

Pair this with some Muscadet or White Bordeaux.

CAVIAR

Pair this with some champagne, preferably vintage.

SWORDFISH

Pair this with some Chardonnay from California or dry Semillons from Australia.

CRAB

Pair this with some Albarino.

SUSHI

Pair this with some Gewürztraminer if it is spicy and Riesling Kabinett if not.

PAIRING WINE WITH CHICKEN:

There are just so many chicken dishes out there waiting to be served with wine. The style of cooking will help in determining the wine that will best suit the dish.

ROAST CHICKEN

Pair this with Red Bordeaux that is mature if the chicken includes all the trimmings. Simple white Bordeaux will do the job for a normal roast.

CHICKEN KIEV

Pair this greasy dish with some Chablis that is acidic.

CHICKEN CASSEROLES

Pair this with Chianti, Sicilian Reds, or Light Merlot.

CHICKEN PIE

Pair this with some Australian Chardonnay.

MORE ABOUT TANNINS

Tannins come from a number of places, including from the grape skins that are used in the making of the wine, as well as from the barrels in which the wine is left to age in. If you want to know what tannin tastes like suck on a teabag - the tastes are very similar. It is the astringency in the tannins that helps to strip off the fats from your tongue and to cleanse your palate after a rich meal. They also provide a drink that is refreshing and refined.

There are studies that indicate that tannin may be able to help cut the risk of coronary heart disease because it may be able to suppress peptide, which causes a hardening of the arteries.

SIX FOODS THAT DON'T PAIR WITH WINE

Some of you may well be filled with rage when you realize that one of your favorite foods may not pair with red wine. We are talking about chocolate and, sadly, the pairing really doesn't work. There are a number of reasons why certain foods will make a wine taste bad and once you know what they are, it will make it much easier for you to select the right wine for the food you are eating. I am going to talk to you about six foods that do not pair well with wines and tell you which wines will actually go with them and, yes, there is a wine for chocolate. First, though, let us just have a look at the difference between a perfect pairing and a terrible pairing:

- **Perfect** – when two of the ingredients combine to create a more balanced and far better-tasting flavor than they do separately.

- **Terrible** - when the combination of ingredients results in something that is unbalanced and clings to your palate or makes you feel ill.

CHOCOLATE

When you taste chocolate, you get a few sensations to the palate, including fattiness, textured tannin, and sweetness, even an earthy flavor. If you pair this with red wine, the wine, or the tannins in it, will simply strip the fat and sweetness from your tongue. This will leave you with nothing more than the harshness of tannin and a sour taste. To make this even worse, the initial fruity flavors of the wine, such as blackberry or cherry, are completely overpowered by the flavor of the chocolate. There may be the odd case where it works, maybe with a white chocolate because this contains no chocolate tannin, but in most cases, if you use the guidelines in the previous chapter for tasting, you will find that all of the components together taste far worse than they do individually.

WINES THAT PAIR WITH CHOCOLATE

The best wines to pair with chocolate are sweet reds. If you are eating truffles or perhaps a chocolate mousse, try a 10-year-old tawny or a vintage port that add an amazing five spice and cinnamon note. If you are contemplating a fruity chocolate dessert, go for a low alcohol Italian sparkling red while a sweet Amarone will match with chocolate and orange.

BRUSSELS SPROUTS

Brussel Sprouts are a member of the cruciferous vegetable family that is nutty, sulfurous, and earthy. Those earthy and sulfurous flavors cause big problems when it comes to pairing with wine. Organosulfur compounds in the vegetable make it difficult to find the right wine simply because they mimic the taste of a wine flaw. You will find the same thing at different levels in cauliflower, garlic, asparagus, and broccoli

WINES THAT PAIR WITH BRUSSELS SPROUTS

There are a couple of wines that will match with a cruciferous vegetable, the best being a dry Madeira wine, served slightly chilled. You can also pair with white or orange biodynamic wines that have a nutty flavor or a nice French Muscadet that has distinct lager tones

ASPARAGUS

The problem with asparagus is similar to the problem with Brussels sprouts, but this time you also have the addition of the chlorophyll in the vegetable, which causes a more distinct herbaceous quality. With many green vegetables, a good zesty white wine will suffice, but with asparagus, it's a little more difficult.

WINES THAT PAIR WITH ASPARAGUS

One of the best pairings for asparagus is a chilled dry sherry because it adds in nutty flavors that are subtle. Try drinking one of these with a cream of asparagus soup and see what you think.

BLUE CHEESE

Cheese and wine go together very well, but Blue cheeses tend to be a little more difficult. This is because it contains alkane-2-ones, an odiferous aroma compound that is also to be found in sphagnum swamp moss. The distinct and strong smell of Blue cheese does tend to have an overpowering effect on most wines.

WINES THAT PAIR WITH BLUE CHEESE

Because of the powerful smell, you need an equally powerful wine that is sweet to act as a counter balance. Port wine is the best to choose as the earthiness of the cheese is eliminated by the acidity of the wine, which in turn brings out the creaminess of the cheese. You could also choose a Shiraz, Zinfandel, or a sweet dessert wine.

SUSHI

Raw fish, sesame, and seaweed combined make it very difficult to pair off with a wine. A Japanese study was carried out to see why fish does not pair with red wine and the results showed that the minute amounts of iron in the wine attach themselves to the oils in the fish and stick to the palate, leaving you with a rather metallic and fishy aftertaste.

Wines that Pair with Sushi

Go for a bone-dry white from a cool climate growing area, like Austria. You could also try a French Muscadet or Sauvignon Blanc, an Italian Pinot Noir, or Brut or Extra Brut champagne.

Soy Sauce

The flavors in soy sauce are produced from soybeans that are fermented, together with salt and wheat. The aroma is reminiscent of wheat berries, and the flavor is bold and salty with a hint of sour. Trying to pair soy sauce with wine that isn't sour will cause the wine to taste somewhat flabby. However, the salty nature of soy sauce can reduce the bitter tannin taste in some wines.

Wines that Pair with Soy Sauce

There are two ways to go here – congruent or complimentary.

- Complimentary – create a sweet and salty pairing by trying a sparkling Moscato.
- Congruent – Add more of the umami by trying an umami-based wine. These come from Languedoc-Roussillon, Southern Rhône, Sadegna, or Southern Italy. This pairing will enhance the fruity flavor of the wines.

CHAPTER SEVENTEEN

FIVE BASIC WINE CHARACTERISTICS

There are five main characteristics of wine:

- Sweetness
- Acidity
- Tannin
- Fruit
- Body

If you can learn to detect these five characteristics, you can learn how to develop your palate, which will help you to determine the best wines and find your favorites. By understanding these characteristics, you will have a much better chance of determining a good wine from a bad wine. This should follow on naturally from learning how to taste; see my chapter on learning how to taste wine like an expert.

SWEETNESS OR LEVEL OF DRYNESS

Human beings perceive sweet tastes when they hit the tip of our tongue. In fact, this will usually be your very first impression. To taste the sweetness of wine, focus all of your attention on those taste buds at the tip of the tongue. Are they tingling? Many dry white wines have a sweet hint that give an impression of a larger body. If you discover that a wine you are fond of has residual sugar it is most likely that you will enjoy a good sweetness to your wine.

HOW TO TASTE SWEETNESS IN YOUR WINE

- Tingling on the tip of the tongue.
- Light oily sensation on the center of the tongue that lingers on.
- Wine has a high viscosity and should tear on the glass gradually; this indicates a higher level of ABV as well.
- Dry reds will occasionally contain 0.9 g/L of sugar, more often the cheaper wines.
- Bone dry wines may be confused with a high tannin wine.

ACIDITY

When you taste an acidic food, it tends to be zesty and tart. With wine, many people confuse acidity with a higher level of alcohol.

It is more common for a wine made from grapes grown in a

cooler climate to be more acidic than those grown in warmer climates are. Acidic wines taste much lighter and spritzy.

Characteristics

- Tingling on the sides and front of the tongue feels a little like the pop rocks or exploding candy
- Rubbing your tongue along the top of your mouth feels somewhat gravelly
- Your mouth feels wetter, a bit like you have just taken a mouthful of a juicy fruit

TANNIN

Tannin tends to be commonly mixed up with the level of dryness in wine because tannin will dry your mouth out. Wine tannins are fond in phenolic compounds that add a taste of bitterness to a wine. Phenolics are present in the seeds and skins of grapes and can also be added when a wine is aged in oak barrels. Tannin tastes like a used tea bag, which is not surprising when you consider that a wet tea bag is almost pure tannin, again with that bitter and drying taste. Tannin can taste herbaceous and has a level of astringency. While this all sounds very negative, tannin adds a measure of complexity, structure, balance, and also makes your wine last longer.

HOW DOES A HIGH TANNIN WINE TASTE?

- Bitter on the side and front of your tongue and mouth
- Leaves you with a dry tongue
- You will have a bitter and dry sensation in your mouth that lingers after you have swallowed the wine

FRUIT

Many wines are characterized by their fruit flavors and it is these that can help you to define your preferences in terms of what you do and don't like. The level of fruitiness is dependent on the different growing regions and climates.

TASTING FOR FRUITINESS IN A WINE

- **Red Wine:** flavors of red fruits like raspberries, strawberries, and darker fruits like blueberries and blackberries.
- **White Wine:** Tastes of lemon, lime, peach, yellow apple.
- You should be able to name at least three fruits that you can distinguish.
- You should be able to easily identify specific fruit flavors.

BODY

Do you want a wine that is light bodied, medium, or full? The body of a wine is dependent on many different factors – the variety, the region it comes from, the vintage, the level of alcohol, and how the wine was made. The body is a snapshot of the overall impression.

ABV – ALCOHOL BY VOLUME

This adds body and the wine will be more viscous. High alcohol wines tend to taste fuller bodied than those that are lower in alcohol.

TASTING BODY IN WINE

- How does this wine compare with others that you have tasted? Does it taste fuller or lighter?
- How long does the taste linger in your mouth after you have swallowed the wine? A couple of seconds? A minute?
- Does the wine taste full bodied to start with but drops off afterward?

CHAPTER EIGHTEEN

HOW TO UNDERSTAND VINTAGE

Vintage is the main thing that many people find very complicated and somewhat confusing. It shouldn't be because, at the end of the day, vintage is very simple – all it tells you is the year that the grapes were harvested. Most still wines will be derived from one single vintage, and the labels on the bottles show you the year the wine was made. There are a couple of exceptions to this rule – wines that are cheap and are really not all that drinkable, and branded wines.

Sparkling and Fortified wines do not tend to have a vintage because they are created by blending a number of vintages with the sole aim of creating a house wine. There is one exception, however, in a particularly outstanding year, you will find vintage ports and champagnes. In both of these, it is down to the produce to determine if the year is good enough to produce one single vintage wine or port. Port is matured for two years in oak barrels before it can be assessed and only after that period will the decision on vintage be made. The conditions have to be spot on to produce a grape that is of a high enough quality to make a vintage champagne, and this tends to mean that we only get a couple of vintages in any decade.

But, why is one vintage so different from another one? Well, the answer to that comes from the weather. Microclimates in particular growing areas vary from year to year, and that change can sometimes be extreme and dramatic. Different varieties of grape respond to different weather conditions in their own unique way. For example, a Shiraz grape will respond well to conditions that are dry and sunny because this helps the sugars in the grape to ripen. The sugar is the main ingredient that gives the wine its alcoholic, heavy kick and that explains why the Barossa Valley wine growers in South Australia have shown great success with Shiraz grapes. A Sauvignon Blanc, on the other hand, prefers a cooler and damper weather climate, thriving very well in the Loire Valley and South Island in New Zealand.

Poor conditions are a real test for any grape grower because they do not suit any particular variety. In these conditions, it is a test of the true mettle of a producer, of his or her experience and knowledge in manipulating the process and blending to produce the best performance possible from the grapes. A really good winemaker will be able to produce good wine from poor grapes, but a mediocre one will only produce an average wine, even with the perfect harvest.

That said, the climate could test the most superior wine makers, in particular, the El Nino cycle. The effect of this is felt more strongly in Australia, and it can produce very unpredictable weather patterns that bring complications for regional growers. In 1993, for example, very heavy rains resulted in a disastrous year for light wines and in 1995 drought-like conditions led to a low yield, although those that did ripen, ripened very well. The weather can work in their favor though. In 1998, a long and warm summer in Australia produced a very exceptional vintage.

CHAPTER NINETEEN

TOP FACTS ABOUT WINE

Wine is one of the oldest and most complex of all alcoholic drinks, with a wonderfully varied and fascinating history. If you started now, it would take you many years to truly understand the intricacies of wine and to become a true connoisseur but you can start by learning a few fascinating facts to sharpen up your brain.

DRINKING WINE CAN VASTLY IMPROVE YOUR SEX LIFE

You might not think this, indeed, you could be forgiven for thinking the complete opposite, but this is one of the most interesting facts about wine. If you drink it regularly, it can work at boosting your sex drive. A study carried out in Italy showed that women who had two glasses of wine every day were much happier in the bedroom than those who did not drink any at all. And that, my friends, is a very good reason to drink wine!

THE CHINESE ARE THE LARGEST CONSUMERS OF RED WINE BUT NOT PER CAPITA

That honor goes to a very small country. The Chinese broke all records by drinking their way through an astonishing 155 million cases of wine, each one containing no less than 9 liters. They overtook the French, a country that most people mistakenly believe are the biggest consumers of red wine, but whose consumption actually dropped by 18% to just 150 million cases. Red wine is becoming hugely popular in China because it is considered to be a very lucky color. The symbolic importance that the Chinese place on red is to do with health, and this is what encourages them to go for red rather than white.

However, they are not the biggest wine consumers in the world per capita. Italy is the largest producer, but they only manage to reach number four on the list. The largest American wine consumers are California, followed closely by New York and then Florida. France does still drink more wine than the Chinese with 53 liters per capita per year, against 1.9 in China, but that includes all wines. The country that drinks the most wine per capita is the Vatican, with a total of 74 liters per capita per year, or around 99 of the 75cl bottles.

WE CAN THANK THE MONKS FOR OUR WINE

Back in the middle ages, Cistercian and Benedictine monks were responsible for preserving winemaking and for innovating it. It is because of the research they did and the efforts that they put in that we have the winemaking technology we enjoy today. The most famous Dom Perignon champagne was named after Dom Pierre Perignon, a monk who lived from 1638 to 1715 and an early advocate for winemaking that was known for experimenting with different methods and for improving the way we make wine. Today, we still use the processes and techniques that he perfected.

NOT ALL WINE IS GOOD FOR YOUR HEALTH

We all know that red wine is supposed to be good for our health. It contains antioxidants, like resveratrol and polyphenol, that help to lower the risk of heart disease and they also have cancer-fighting properties. Grape skin is very rich in antioxidants, especially that which comes off the red grape and, as red wine is made from grapes fermented in their skins, it has a higher level of antioxidants than white skin, which is fermented without the skins. White wine has been reported to raise the risk of cancer slightly, especially in the digestive tract, so it is best to stick to a maximum of one or two glasses per day.

The Name of a Wine Generally Indicates its Region

Many wines from Europe are named after the geographical location that they are grown in. One famous example of this is the Bordeaux wine, which is made from grapes grown in the Bordeaux region in France. Bordeaux wines are made for a number of different varieties of grape, including the Cabernet Franc, Cabernet Sauvignon, Petit Verdot, Merlot, and Malbec, and Carmenere to a smaller extent.

Non-European wines tend to carry the name of the grape variety instead, for example, the Californian wine Cabernet Sauvignon.

You Can Tell the Geographical Location of a Wine by its Color

This is very true – a darker wine shade, i.e., dark reds and dark yellow whites, originate from warmer climates while the lighter reds and whites come from cooler climates.

Women Get Drunk on Wine Quicker than Men

This is because of their ratio of fat to water, nothing whatsoever to do with how much they weigh or how big they are. If a woman and a man, both of equal size and build, were to drink the same quantity of wine, the woman would have a much higher blood alcohol content than the man. This is because the woman and women in general, have a much higher fat content than men do, and fat will not absorb the alcohol. As such, the alcohol will be unable to dilute itself as much, and that leads to a much higher blood alcohol content.

WINE WAS FIRST DISCOVERED IN THE MIDDLE EAST AROUND 6000 YEARS AGO

The very first remnants of wine were found in Iran and dated back to the Neolithic period, which ran from 8500 to 4000 BC. As far as cultivated wines go, the earliest example was found in Georgia and dates to somewhere between 7000 and 5000 BC. Native yeast came into contact with stored grapes accidentally and caused a fermentation that was not deliberately performed. The sugars in the grapes turned into alcohol and the Egyptians later refined this process, before being spread across the Mediterranean by the Greeks. It was made popular over Europe by the Romans and, following that, the Spanish and other Europeans took the brew to the New World, South Africa, and Oceania.

WINE REALLY DOESN'T MAKE YOU FAT

We all know that beer causes a beer belly, something that does not really look all that attractive but, contrary to popular belief, wine does not have any adverse effects on your waistline. Recent studies have shown that women who drink wine on a regular basis, in moderate amounts (one drink per day) actually carried approximately 10 pounds less body fat than those who did not drink. Experts say that alcohol calories do not go through the same metabolism process as food calories, so they do not gather as fat in our bodies. So, if you are considering a diet to lose weight, perhaps you should consider a glass of wine for dessert instead of something else.

THE TERM TOAST IS OLDER THAN WE THINK

In fact, it originated back in Ancient Rome. At the time, the Senate declared that Emperor Augustus was to be honored at every single meal with a toast. The custom started with a slice of toast that was burnt, called Tostus, which was dropped into the wine. It was believed that this was done as a way of masking the taste of the wine, which was unpleasant, and was the original and ancient method of soaking. Every person at the table would raise their glass to the Emperor, thus giving rise to the well-known custom of today. But, in those days, treachery was everywhere, and poisoning became the most common way for debts to be paid off. It became a custom that hosts would toast each guest before every meal, and they would drink the wine from a common bowl just to show that it had not been poisoned.

FEAR OF WINE

Believe it or not, there is such a thing. While it isn't too common, wine can really put fear into a few unlucky souls. It's called Oenophobia, and the official definition is "the fear of wine; anxiety related to wine."

TUTANKHAMUN LABELED HIS WINE

Tutankhamun, the boy king who died in 1325 BC, liked a glass of red and, when his tomb was opened in 1922, archeologists found a number of wine jars. Each one was clearly labeled with the name of the wine, the year of harvest, the source or region and the name of the vine grower. In fact, the labels had so much detail on them that they would have passed the modern laws regarding labeling in several countries. Unsurprisingly, the wine in the jars had dried by the time it was found. However, a team of Spanish scientists ran tests and were able to confirm that the jars had held red wine by picking out the remnants of an acid that is found in red wine.

SYMPOSIUMS ARE NOT WHAT YOU THINK

We have always thought of symposiums as being a meeting of professionals or business academics to debate current affairs or to discuss their profession. You would be right if you thought that, but it is also just a big excuse to have a drink. The term "symposium" came from Ancient Greece and it translates literally into "drinking together," which reflects the love that the Greeks had, and still do, of mixing an evening of intellectual discussion with a few drinks.

Symposia were held in the male quarters of a household and those invited would be invited to relax on couches piled high with pillows, while food, wine, and entertainment were served up for them. At the same time, they would spend the evening discussing philosophy and politics. These meetings were also held to introduce a new young man into aristocratic society.

The symposiums would be overseen by a "symposiarch", the ancient version of today's modern sommelier and it would be they who determined the strength of the wine for the evening. Their choice was based on the topics being discussed and on how serious the discussion would be. The wine would be served mixed with water because it was considered an uncivilized habit to drink pure wine.

AND FINALLY
A few statistics to end the book:

A STANDARD ACRE OF GRAPEVINES PRODUCES:
- Five tons of grapes

- Equal to 3,985 bottles of wine
- Equal to 797 gallons of wine
- Equal to 15,940 glasses of wine
- Or 13 ½ barrels of wine

ONE BARREL OF WINE IS EQUAL TO:
- 1.180 glasses of wine
- Or 24.6 cases of wine

ONE CASE OF WINE IS EQUAL TO:
- 30 lbs. of grapes
- 48 glasses of wine
- 12 bottles of wine

ONE BOTTLE OF WINE IS EQUAL TO:
- 2.4 lbs. of grapes
- 4 glasses of wine
- 4 very happy people!

CHAPTER TWENTY

FINE AND RARE WINES

FINE WINE: CAN YOU DESCRIBE IT?

Fine wines can be compared to a dignified, older woman you set eyes on across the room – who is she and what makes her so appealing? In this section we are going to explore the world of fine wines and what defines one.

WHAT IS A FINE WINE?

There is no one conclusive definition of what constitutes a fine wine; indeed, there are numerous bewildering terms and names for wines but the majority of people cannot define what a fine wine actually is? When looking online, a search for fine wines instantaneously takes you to a website to learn about establishing your own fine wines which costs upwards of £20/$30, so let us begin with establishing a wine collection first and then move onto price.

COLLECTING AND ESTABLISHING YOUR CELLAR

A fine wine is not just something to be admired in a glass or as it swirls around in your mouth, it is something that is valuable and worthy of being within a collection. Although a collection of fine wines is typically linked with how rare they are – such as Le Pin – in reality it is more connected with how well a bottle is able to age. This certainly leaves out many particular styles of wine, including rose wine, but with several fine wines they can be left in a cellar and they will develop and age. Once it has become a collectable item, it then becomes coveted. The desire for this bottle grows and due to limited availability, it then becomes a 'fine wine' with an inflated price tag to go with it.

PRICE

When asked whether price comes into a factor, it was undisputed that aspect as to determine whether a particular wine can be classed as a 'fine wine'. However, it should be stressed that many experts cannot agree as to where the starting point is on this. It appears that it comes down to the level of experience the buyer has in addition to the amount of money they have at their disposal.

A MATTER OF TASTE

Since we all have different tastes (we all have a different amount of taste buds on our tongues), a fine wine can be determined through taste. However, what you may consider fine could actually be disgusting or bland to someone else. This is why the Wine and Spirit Education Trust established a chart in order for the purchaser to evaluate each different wine impartially. There are a number of different issues with this chart, including the fact that it doesn't include a wine's age, price, or even its context.

STATUS

A number of wine experts agree that in order to gain fine wine status, it must be agreed by several independent experts that it meets expectations. These experts can have a great deal of influence on the status and reputation of vineyards and in some ways could be compared to works of fine art.

PROVENANCE AND PEDIGREE

It should be stressed that a fine wine is required to be created with the utmost care and quality in mind. Although experts are hesitant to use terminology such as handcrafted due to the debates on whether machines harvesting the vines are considered appropriate or not, it is generally accepted that methods which reduce the amount of wine being created typically guide the wines produced into the fine wine category. A long pedigree and history, along with names, and excellent vineyard location are also described as evidence for a fine wine. However, there are times when a fine wine emerges onto the scene without being a textbook case, such as Sassicaia or Pingus. Winemakers who use new techniques to create a fantastic product can also work their way into the fine wine classification.

A DEFINITION OF FINE WINE

It is clear that to be considered a fine wine, it must feature all the aspects previously discussed. However, because enjoyment of wine is an individual choice, the definition of what makes a fine wine can be a personal thing. When several experts were asked, they defined a fine wine as something that was worth investing themselves into it, whether it was through locating the wine, storing it, allowing it to age and when it was time to be opened.

Deciding on what makes a wine fine or not comes down to the drinker.

HOW TO BUY FINE WINE – FIVE ESSENTIAL TIPS

The world of fine wine can be exhilarating but if it is something you are just learning about then it can be quite a daunting and scary journey. Where do you begin and what type of wine do you purchase? Read the following to discover five essential tips on how to buy fine wine.

ASK FOR ADVICE

From little stores to expansive merchants, there is a vast number of experts, traders, and merchants who are more than happy to help you. Over the years, these people have amassed a great deal of information on fine wines, from long-established winemakers to newly established brands.

TRY A COSTLIER STYLE OF SOMETHING YOU ALREADY ENJOY

One of the easiest ways to develop your experience in fine wines is to try a more expensive style or brand of wine that you already like. Try to compare the two versions. Instead of spending $15 on a bottle of Merlot, try spending $35 and find out if you can taste the difference between the two bottles.

KEEP TO A BUDGET AND MAKE NOTES

Expanding your practical knowledge of fine wine can get to be an expensive hobby so it is important that you set yourself a budget and stick to it. Once a bottle has been opened, make notes about what you liked and what you didn't like about it. Compare the notes for each bottle with previous notes; this is a great way of finding out if you prefer a particular region or grape, allowing you to ignore the types that you don't particularly enjoy.

ENJOY WITH OTHERS

If you have a friend or perhaps several friends who are interested in expanding their knowledge of fine wine, then you have a great way of enjoying it. Once a month, have a big get together where everyone brings a bottle and not only will you get the chance to sample several fine wines instead of just one, you'll also have fun doing so!

USE EXPERT WEBSITES

There are a number of good online resources where you can gain access to a vast amount of knowledge on fine wines. Many have dedicated experts available to help you work your way through the extensive listings and provide you with the best choice. In a short time, you will be able to go through them on your own without having a professional help you.

ESTABLISHING A FINE WINE CELLAR: EIGHT TOP TIPS

In Hong Kong in 2014, a collection of 114 bottles of fine wine (Romanee-Conti wine, to be exact) were sold at auction at a staggering price of HK $12.5 million (over £1 million or $1.6 million), making this the most expensive wine collection to be purchased in the world.

It should be stressed, however, that deals like the Hong Kong one are the exception but even still, anyone in the wine industry will tell you that collecting wine, whether it is for love or for money, is an exhilarating and passionate pastime.

Whether you are establishing a fine wine cellar for passion or for money, here are the top eight tips you should know.

BE READY TO PAY OUT

The first tip when establishing a fine wine collection is to be ready to pay out. Starting out your own collection is quite an expensive hobby for several reasons. Not only do you have to pay out for the wine itself, but then you need to invest in a decent storage unit, a catalogue system or subscription, some sort of security system and up to date insurance. Your best bet is to draw up a budget and stick to it in order not to overspend.

KNOWLEDGE IS POWER

As any teacher will tell you, the key to your future is knowledge. Apply this to your fine wine cellar. If you don't have much knowledge on the qualities of what makes a wine 'fine' then now is the time to educate yourself. Occasionally, the label on the bottle will tell you how long you should cellar it for but sometimes this is an over-estimation and you may end up with a wine that tastes somewhat like vinegar.

WHERE DOES IT COME FROM?

The quality of your wine can largely depend on where it comes from. For example, if the bottle of wine has been left to sit somewhere it shouldn't be, such as in the front window of a store, then it may not taste as good as it should have and may not be worth to continue aging.

CATALOGUE

It is important that when establishing your fine wine cellar that you should invest in a decent catalogue system. Begin with the first bottle of wine you purchase and carry on with each other you buy. There are a number of decent subscriptions which allow you to make notes and track every bottle, along with the handy alert features which informs you of what wines you already have.

KEEP YOUR RECORDS

It is also important that you keep all the documents and proof of purchase of every bottle you buy. This could be the receipt, the auction catalogue and everything else that has details of the wine you have purchased. If you decide to sell it onwards, or if there is something wrong with it, then you will need all of these records.

STORE IT AS IT SHOULD BE

Wine is like a decent woman – you need to treat her right if you want a good outcome. Fine wine needs to be looked after, being stored away in a cool and humid location where the temperature is consistent, as is the lighting. As such, a basement is the perfect place to store it. Wine bottles should be facing down instead of standing straight up. If you can, keep your wine in their original boxes as this will help if you decide to re-sell them.

As your wine gets older, it likes to be left alone (somewhat like a cranky old man), so whilst it may be tempting to go in, pull out a bottle and admire it, it is best to leave it alone. Once the time has come to open it, then you will reap your rewards.

BUY THE WINES YOU WANT TO ENJOY

Another great tip is to purchase the wines that you actually want to enjoy. As with a lot of fashion trends, wine fashions will vary from year to year. Some of these trends will allow for new encounters and innovations to emerge but the truth is that your collection's monetary worth will vary conditionally on the time.

The only way you can ensure you have a great collection is by purchasing the wines that you genuinely want to enjoy.

PATIENCE

One of the greatest parts of a fine wine collection is when you finally open a bottle up and enjoy the contents. However, to get to this point takes a lot of dedication and patience. You will undoubtedly encounter occasions when you have a group of friends or family over one night and try to encourage you in any way they can to open one of your more expensive bottles of wine. However, keep calm and resist the urge to give into their pleas.

KNOW YOUR WINE IMPERFECTIONS

Faults in your wine, especially when it comes to corked wine, can be incredibly annoying and put you off a brand at time. However, the majority of wine merchants will happily exchange it for a new bottle. Cork taint can be hard to tell for those just getting their feet wet in the world of wine so it is best that you educate yourself on what could actually be wrong with your wine. However, it should be noted that sometimes a wine may just not taste right due to your own personal taste.

Let's now take a look at several ways you can tell if you have something wrong with your bottle of wine.

CORK TAINT (ALSO KNOWN AS TRICHLOROANISOLE)

One of the most popular corked wine myths is that it refers to small pieces of cork which have come apart and are floating about in your wine. On the contrary, it actually refers to the existence of a chemical taint known as 2, 4, 6-Trichloroanisole (or TCA in its shorten form). Most of the time, it occurs from the actual cork but it can occur within oak barrels and bottle lines. Regardless of how it occurs, it will taint the full batch of wine, not just a singular bottle. This chemical taint, however, is not dangerous – it just makes the wine taste bad.

You can spot cork taint by smelling the wine – if it tastes as though an entire room has been infested with mold, or wet cardboard, then you have cork taint.

OXIDATION

Oxidation is where the grape juice has been exposed to more oxygen than needed and has gone bad. For example, if you open a bottle of wine, drink a single glass of wine and then leave it on the side for several days and then take another drink, you can notice the difference. The wine has been exposed to too much oxygen and the fresh, vibrant flavor has now been lost. It can also happen when damage has occurred to the cork or bottle top, or if it hasn't been sealed properly.

However, it should be stressed that sometimes the winemakers will oxidize their wines on purpose in order to create a distinctive style of wine.

The best way to spot oxidation in your wine is by the color of the liquid. Red wines will turn brownish or brackish in tone, whereas whites will take on an amber or brownish hue. Both red and white wines will start to take on a bitter taste.

REDUCTION

Reduction is the opposite to oxidization; it is where it hasn't been exposed to the right amount of oxygen needed as it was being made. Oxidation is something to be avoided at all costs by winemakers and they will go to all lengths to avoid or counter it; unfortunately, sometimes this results in the opposite direction and reduction is the outcome.

The best way to tell that a bottle of your wine has been spoiled by reduction is by smelling it – if it gives off an aroma of rotten eggs or of sulphur, then it's likely that the wine has suffered from this process.

Even if your wine has suffered from reduction, there is a chance of saving it. You can decant the wine or drop a (clean) copper coin into the wine.

HIGH MEASURES OF VOLATILE ACIDITY (VA)

Volatile acidity, or VA in its shorten form, is manifested naturally and when there is just a trace of it, it can enhance the taste of the wine. A number of winemakers will actually put a trace of it into the wine to give it new depths but in higher quantities it tastes somewhat similar to vinegar. It is from the bacteria in the wine which produces the acetic acid.

You can spot whether your bottle of wine has high measures of volatile acidity if it gives off an aroma somewhat like vinegar or nail varnish remover. If tasted, it will taste somewhat like vinegar as well.

RE-FERMENTATION

This fault is where red or white wines have become fizzy when they shouldn't have. This fizziness comes about when the residual sugar comes into contact with the remaining yeast once it has been poured into the bottles. The majority of this occurrence is when the sweeter wines have become tainted with bacteria in unsterile environments.

Obviously, the best way to spot this fault is by seeing little bubbles in your wine when they should not be there. However, some wines are meant to have bubbles so make sure you have the right wine!

CHAPTER TWENTY ONE

FINE WINE VINEYARDS

What defines a fine wine comes down to personal choice, but where it comes from (as we have already discussed) will also be a contributing factor. Certain vineyards have enjoyed solid reputations for producing fine wines for centuries, others for around a century whilst some have just emerged onto the scene.

In this chapter we will be looking at a number of different vineyards from around the world who enjoy a reputation as manufacturers of fine wines.

KAPCSANDY

Located in Yountville in the south of Napa Valley, USA, the family run Kapcsandy vineyard have created a number of outstanding fine wines, gaining a reputation for producing rare and high-class wines which are hard to come by in California.

Owning 15.5 acres, they produce between 2,500 and 4,000 cases of wine annually, with each one being sought after.

Kapcsandy was originally known as the Beringer State Line Vineyard but the name was changed when it was brought by the new owners in 2000. The old vineyard had suffered much due to phylloxera and new grapes had to be replanted; the new vines were planted to maximize growing potential.

Kapcsandy produces a number of fine wines but their Kapcsandy Estate Cuvee is quite exceptional. It consists of a blending of merlot and cabernet sauvignon; other distinctive wines include the Roberta's Reserve and the Cabernet Sauvignon Grand Vin State Line Vineyard which features around 90% Cabernet Sauvignon.

The majority of the cases produced are reserved for purchasers who are on a waiting list and what remains is then distributed for the rest of the world market.

PENFOLDS GRANGE

The Penfolds Grange vineyard opened in 1951 and has since then become one of the leading wine producers in the entire world. Located in South Australia, it is extremely popular that it has been awarded a Heritage Icon status. A Borossa Shiraz which leads in any Australian wine, has become a fundamental part of all fine wine cellars.

Penfolds Grange has taken the iconic Shiraz grape, along with a limited amount of Cabernet Sauvignon, and created a blend which illustrates the distinctions of that vintage. Taking the best quality grapes from the southern part of the country, every single bottle of their wine is something to be proud to own.

In 1955, Penfolds Grange was awarded with the title of the Wine of the Century by Wine Spectacular, beating numerous other well-established vineyards around the world.

SINE QUA NON

In recent times, Sine Qua Non has been hailed as the most collectable fine wine in the world, being one of the most exclusive vineyards in California. In the beginning of the 2000s under the owner, Manfred Krankl, the vineyard hit its highest peak, producing some exquisite blends that have been praised all over the world by leading experts and wine and lifestyle magazines. On the world market, very few fine wines can dare to compete with it when it comes to being desired.

The vineyard uses Grenache and Syrah grapes originated from the Rhone area, as well as other varieties, each blend is something to be desired and coveted. This is especially true since purchasing the wine is extremely tight and only through the estate's mailing list.

BEAUJOLAIS NOUVEAU

The Beaujolais Nouveau wine is highly popular with fine wine lovers but unlike other blends which takes a longer fermentation stage, this one enjoys a quicker process which gives the drinker a fresher and vibrant taste.

The vineyard is located in the French region of Beaujolais and was founded around 100 years ago. Instead of being established with producing a fine wine, the owners intended it to create a cheaper yet enjoyable beverage for the natives of the area to enjoy once the harvest season had finished.

The vineyard's success in enjoying a high-class reputation is largely down to Georges Duboeuf. A new idea was brought to life – whether the Beaujolais Nouveau wine could be the first to arrive in Paris over the other brands and the media went wild over it. During the 1970s, the race was being enjoyed all over the country; in the 1980s, other European countries were taking notice and then by America and Asia in the following decades.

Originally, the motto for the marketing of the Beaujolais Nouveau wine was "the Beaujolais Nouveau wine has arrived" but in 2005 it was altered to "its Beaujolais Nouveau time!"

Whilst other fine wines are meant to be left to age, Beaujolais Nouveau wine is supposed to be enjoyed whilst it is still young. However, certain vintages can be left to age until desired.

LE PIN

Le Pin, which was established in 1979, has enjoyed one of the finest reputations for the production of fine wines in the world. WSJ once quoted, *"It took Bordeaux centuries to create great wine, Jacques Thienpont did it in just 30 years"*.

Le Pin originates from small and humble origins. The land had been in the hands of the Loubie family since the 1920s and the wine produced from them was known as Pomerol. When Jacques Thienpont purchased the land in 1979, who was from Belgium and his family worked in the wine industry since the 1840s, he re-named the vineyard Le Pin and then expanded the land by purchasing small parcels of land from neighboring owners. He concentrated on enhancing his skills and expanding his knowledge and in 1982, he made headlines with his delectable new vintage and has carried on improving and producing outstanding new blends.

Perhaps one of Le Pin's successes can be due to the relatively small number of cases he produces each year. He created between 600 and 700 cases of wine on an annual basis which, when compared to other winemakers who can produce upwards of 29,000 cases annually, this makes his wines quite rare. This certainly makes any of his wines desirable and something many collectors covet.

Another key factor in his success is that experts believe the soil in which his vines grow contributes to the taste of the wine. The soil in which his grapes grow consist of a sandy consistency which sits upon a limestone bedrock; the soil in which his neighbors grow their vines in is quite different to Le Pin's, which makes his wine unique to theirs.

The price of Le Pin's wines have certainly taken off in recent years which has led it to be in competition with Petrus for the label of the world's most expensive wine. A case of his 1982 blend originally cost around £200/$300 but today it is over £50,000/$75,000.

CHATEAU MARGAUX

Bordeaux wine has longed enjoyed a reputation for being an outstanding location for rich Bordeaux wine. However, Chateau Margaux is perhaps the most illustrious and famous producer of wine in the Bordeaux region of France.

Chateaux Margaux first began its production of wine in the 18th century but in 1787 had become one of the most famous winemakers in the world. It did experience a decline in fortunes during the French Revolution period and the following few years but by the early 20th century it regained its reputation when the Mentzelopoulous family took control of it. Since then, it has continued to produce excellent vintages which highlight the grace and sophistication of the Bordeaux region.

The Margaux wine has often been described by experts as enjoying a delicate and elegant flavor, one that entices the drinker to savor each aroma and sip. The blending of specific berries and flowers produces an intoxicating and mesmerizing beverage which sets it apart from other Bordeaux wines in the area.

Chateaux Margaux owns 82 hectares of land, 75% of which consists of Cabernet Sauvignon, 20% of Merlot, and the remaining land by other varieties. The Grand Vin and the Pavilion Blanc de Chateaux Margaux blends are highly desirable to collectors.

CONCLUSION

Getting to grips with the wine game can be an intimidating process. There are so many different wines from all over the world – good, bad, indifferent, and even downright ugly. Then there are sparkling and fortified wines to complicate things further, so how do you go about choosing something you'll enjoy, that won't decimate your budget for the month?

If you strip away the fanciful descriptions used by some celebrity critics and get back to basics, it can be surprisingly simple, and even pleasurable, to choose a wine you'll enjoy and want to return to again and again.

You should have some idea whether your preference is for dry, medium, or sweet wines; red, white, or rose; oaked or unoaked; aged or young. If you don't, you need to read up on some wines and attend some tastings, so you can get an idea of the basic styles of wine you enjoy and begin to educate your palate. Take advice from people who know – Sommeliers, wine merchants, knowledgeable sales assistants, and respected critics. Wine tastes are subjective, so going on customer reviews may not be helpful, unless those customers are particularly knowledgeable, and you have no way of knowing that.

Above all, don't get too bogged down in the whole thing. Wine drinking is both a pleasure and a privilege, and the main thing is that you enjoy it. If it is a good vintage, or an award-winning wine, that's a bonus, but remember it's all about the taste. Everything else is secondary. If you enjoy a cheap bottle of wine from the bargain basement in the liquor store, it's a good wine as far as you are concerned. On the other hand, if you find an award-winning wine is not to your taste, it's a bad wine, regardless of what the critics say about it.

Wine drinking at its best is subjective and personal, and it's to be enjoyed. Don't be intimidated – get out there, try the wines, learn what you like and drink it as often as you can. Don't be put off when you find a wine you love, just because it isn't in the top 20 for the season or vintage. Enjoy it – that's why wine was invented, and that's why it's still enjoyed all over the world, thousands of years later!

BONUS!

Do you love wine and premium wine products? If so, we want to invite you to Xtrend's mailing list to receive super deals on Xtrend's newest products, coming out every month!

… **You will also receive great wine content, free wine guides, and much more!**

Click here to be the first person to hear about all the newest products, super discounts and the most up-to-date premium wine related content!

Get Super Discounts --→ Xtrend – The Wine Loving Company

Link: https://xtrend.leadpages.co/xtrend

We never spam. We never send out anything that does not provide value. We respect you absolutely.